ZX81 BASIC Book

Robin Norman

Howard W. Sams & Co., Inc.
4300 WEST 62ND ST. INDIANAPOLIS, INDIANA 46268 USA

FIRST EDITION
SECOND PRINTING — 1982

First published in the United Kingdom by Newnes Technical Books, an imprint of the Butterworth Group. Americanized version published by Howard W. Sams & Co., Inc.
Indianapolis, IN 46268

International Standard Book Number:
(United Kingdom Edition) 0-408-01178-5
(North American Edition) 0-672-21957-3
Library of Congress Catalog Card Number: 82-50022

North American Edition
Edited by: *Jim Rounds*
Illustrated by: *Wm. D. Basham*

Printed in the United States of America.

PREFACE

It's hard for a mere author to keep up with the microcomputer industry. In 1980 I wrote a book for new owners of the Sinclair ZX80, and simultaneously with the publication of that book, the latest Sinclair offering was announced — the ZX81. ZX80 was an incredible machine, but it did leave one saying, "If only it would do this and this . . .". Now nearly all these gaps have been well and truly filled by the Sinclair ZX81, which does nearly everything for less money!

The reception for our previous book was good enough to encourage Newnes and myself to press on with a new version for the ZX81. With so many new features available in ZX81 BASIC, it was obvious that most of the book would have to be rewritten. Nevertheless we have used the same layout, and made the same three assumptions about the reader of the book — who naturally may be "she" or "he":

1. He is a newcomer to computer programming (depending on experience, he can of course skip early sections of the book).
2. He has one particular microcomputer, the Sinclair ZX81, switched on, in front of him.
3. He wants to learn to use all the instructions in ZX81 BASIC, using a structured course with a steadily increasing tempo.

You cannot "read" a book like this. Whatever you get out of it will be the result of a three-way interaction between you, this book, and the ZX81. And if you ever find yourself thinking, "What would happen if . . ?" then for goodness sake try it! You won't break the ZX81 and you'll probably learn something.

A few acknowledgments — first to Betty Clare for typing difficult manuscripts so well. To Peter Chapman for helpful ideas, and to my family for still being patient. And finally to Clive Sinclair for lending the hardware — one has to say that with the ZX81 he has "done it again." A marvelous little machine, admittedly a little low on memory (that's what the 16K RAM expansion is for), fine for beginners and yet able to hold its own with many machines costing much more.

Happy programming to you all!

ROBIN NORMAN

Contents

CHAPTER 1

What Do Computers Do?

Rather a philosophical chapter, this — come back to it later if you're in a hurry to get started!

MACHINES CONTROLLING MACHINES

Man is in many respects a poor match for other inhabitants of this planet. We have achieved our dominance on Earth because of our large brains, and the way in which we have used these to devise tools. These tools not only save labor, but they also allow us to do things that would be inconceivable without them.

At some stage in prehistory, we used our flint knife to cut notches on a stick — now we had two different kinds of tool:

(1) Tools to do mechanical work — helping our muscles.
(2) Tools to calculate and remember — helping our brain.

Luckily, we did not put these two kinds of tool into watertight compartments. Our best progress has been made since we combined the two and used the calculating tools to control the mechanical tools. It's been going on for a long time, as these examples will suggest.

Simple gauges to check that arrows are of a standard length and diameter.

Capstan lathes to allow intricate metal working to be done by unskilled people.

Electronically controlled robots to assemble car bodies with a minimum of human help.

Of course, it's electronics and the famous "silicon chip" which have spread automatic control of machines so widely. They also bring social problems to be solved — how to share out the benefits fairly among us all — but that's another story.

"PURE" CALCULATING MACHINES

Since this group includes the Space Invader machine, I thought it best to put the word "pure" in quotes! I use it to mean calculating machines which are not used for the direct control of any other machine. We've been using these for a good long time, for counting our money and possessions, for advancing our knowledge, and to amuse ourselves. Here again the silicon chip has brought about a revolution in reducing the size and price of these machines, until we can get a pocket calculator with pocket money and a microcomputer for a birthday present.

DEDICATED OR OPEN-MINDED

I want to distinguish two different kinds of electronic calculating machines:

(1) The dedicated machine which has a detailed set of instructions built in to make it do one particular job (e.g., Electronic Mastermind).
(2) The machine with an open mind — we can put in our own instructions to make it do all sorts of jobs — including playing a game of Mastermind (e.g., The Sinclair ZX81).

Even the open-minded machines are dedicated to some extent. For instance, the ZX81 has a lot of instructions built in so that it can understand one particular programming language — BASIC.

HARDWARE AND SOFTWARE

There's a lot of jargon used in the computer business — it's a shorthand which helps people on the inside, but forms a barrier to people on the outside. I'll try to keep it to a minimum, and I'll help you by including a glossary of new words (and old words with new meanings) at the end of this book.

Hardware means all the physical parts of the computer — the ZX81, tv set and cassette recorder.

Software means all the programs and instruction books needed to make the computer work — the ZX81 operating manual, this book, the permanent programs put into the ZX81 by its designers, and the programs that you write.

Having gone from the general to the particular, we'll move on to see how we can communicate with a computer.

CHAPTER 2

Talking to Computers

COMPUTER LANGUAGES

Humans have ten fingers, and so have got used to counting in the *decimal* system using the digits 0 to 9. Computers, on the other hand, work with *binary numbers.* A binary digit (bit for short) can only have the values 0 or 1, and the computer is just about bright enough to tell the difference between them!

One can write programs in binary numbers (in the early days of computers this was the only way), but humans find binary numbers clumsy to handle and hard to recognize. A better way is to write programs in a *low-level language,* using machine code based on hexadecimal (base 16) numbers, which are easily converted to binary. Machine code programs are fast to run and economical on computer memory, but they are no way for beginners to learn programming. Most people converse with computers in a *high-level language,* which uses decimal numbers and sets of recognizable English words. Some common high-level languages are:

FORTRAN	FORmula TRANslation, mainly for science and engineering
COBOL	COmmercial Business Oriented Language
BASIC	Beginners All-purpose Symbolic Instruction Code

New languages appear from time to time, having various advantages claimed for them. BASIC is probably the most widely used language in today's generation of microcomputers.

The computer cannot understand these high-level languages on its own, and so programs are built in to translate them via machine code into binary numbers.

COMPUTER MEMORIES

The memories of a computer consist of a large number of "boxes" or "pigeon-holes," each containing an 8-bit binary number (called a *byte*). Memory size is specified in terms of K, where 1K is a memory with a capacity of 1024 bytes. There are two kinds of memory in a microcomputer like the ZX81:

READ ONLY MEMORY (ROM)

This contains the program needed to run the computer and to translate the BASIC instructions into binary code. ROM is permanent and so is not lost when the computer is switched off. The ZX81 uses BASIC in 8K of ROM.

RANDOM ACCESS MEMORY (RAM)

This contains all the data and programs that you put in. It is not permanent, and if you switch the power off for a moment, the RAM contents are lost. Your ZX81 has 1K of RAM available, but you can increase this to 16K by plugging in the 16K RAM pack.

INPUT AND OUTPUT

We need to be able to put data and instructions into the computer memory, and the ZX81 provides us with a scaled-down version of a standard typewriter keyboard for this purpose. We also have to provide the means for the ZX81 to display its results, and for us to see what we are typing in — an ordinary vhf tv set is used for this.

If we want a permanent record of a program, or of the ZX81 output, we can use a printer that is connected to the ZX81. ZX81 uses a non-standard character set, and the only suitable printer is Sinclair's own (at the time of writing this is not yet available).

LONG TERM STORAGE

We've already seen that when you switch off the ZX81, all the contents of the RAM are lost — possibly a precious program that you've taken hours to write! Even if it was recorded on the printer you would have to type it out again. We need long term or *backup storage,* in which to keep our programs and data permanently. ZX81 uses a standard type or cassette recorder, and programs and data can be saved on tape, kept as long as you like, and then loaded back into the ZX81.

LOOKING INTO THE FUTURE

This is the crystal-ball department, a list of the features I should like in my own personal computer in the future:

(1) Greater agreement on standards, so that programs become more interchangeable and computers can talk to each other more easily.
(2) Communication with the computer by voice, both for input and output.
(3) Cheap printed output — preferably in the form of an electronic typewriter which doubles as a printer.
(4) Cheap, unlimited, permanent memory for back up storage.
(5) High-definition output in color, comparable with tv standards.
(6) A large range of cheap software — programs for business, home, learning and leisure — in simple plug-in form.
(7) Connection to large central computers, probably via the tv network, to give access to virtually unlimited information on any chosen subject.

CHAPTER 3

Programming in BASIC

BASIC is one of the most widely used high-level languages, especially for the present generation of microcomputers. There are many different versions of BASIC, in the same way as there are different dialects of English. But do not despair! All versions of BASIC are easily recognizable as coming from the same original source (BASIC was developed at Dartmouth College, New Hampshire), and when you have learned one form of BASIC you can quickly transfer to another form on another computer. Sinclair ZX81 BASIC in 8K ROM is a fairly complete version with a few nonstandard features, and in many ways it is an excellent BASIC for beginners to learn.

THE FIRST COMPUTER PROGRAM?

Let's use a light-hearted example for our first look at programming. Walt Disney's *Fantasia* is revived from time to time, and one of my favorite parts is *The Sorcerer's Apprentice* by Dukas. Mickey Mouse is the apprentice who is left on his own with the boring job of filling a great tank with water from the well. Mickey is a bright lad, and he decides to program one of the kitchen brooms to do the work, while he has a crafty snooze.

When writing a computer program, it's very important to get the instructions in the right order, and so every one is given a number. Mickey's first attempt could have been like this:

1 Pick up bucket and go to well
2 Fill bucket with water
3 Carry bucket to water tank
4 Empty bucket into tank

So far, so good. One bucketful of water has been shifted! Mickey could repeat the same instructions over and over again, numbering them 5, 6, 7, 8, and 9, 10, 11, 12, and so on. Not a bit! He has read Chapter 12 in the spell book, and all he does is to add one more instruction:

---

5 GO TO 1

---

and now he has made a *program loop.* The broom follows the program exactly, and goes happily backwards and forwards, filling and emptying buckets, while Mickey nods off . . .

* * * * *

. . . until he wakes with a start some time later to find water lapping round his knees. You've guessed it — he forgot to tell the broom when to stop! Panic — he chops the broom into sixteen pieces, but each of these gets up and carries on with the work. Luckily the sorcerer returns home just in time. He is skilled in the arts of programming brooms, and knows that every loop must include a "get out" test, or it will go on forever. This vital step always contains the magic word "IF", and we call it a conditional jump.

With its IF statement, and a little renumbering, the final program looks like this:

1 Pick up bucket and go to well
2 Fill bucket with water
3 Carry bucket to water tank
4 Empty bucket into tank
5 IF water tank is not full THEN GO TO 1
6 Report "Tank Full"
7 Stop

The IF statement has to be inside the loop, so that every time the broom goes around the loop, it can check whether the tank is full, and take action accordingly.

Well, that was childish stuff, but it did raise four points which will be important when we come to write real programs for the ZX81.

(1) A BASIC program is made up of a series of *instructions.*
(2) The instructions are all *numbered* so that the computer can carry them out in the order it is told to.
(3) You can make a computer do part of a program over and over again by using a GO TO instruction. We call this a *loop.*
(4) A loop must contain a *conditional jump,* which will stop the computer or send it out of the loop when the condition is obeyed. The magic word is ''IF''!

CHAPTER 4

The Hardware

Before connecting up the hardware and switching on the power, you had better consult Chapter 1 in your manual, *ZX81 BASIC PROGRAMMING*. The three vital parts are the ZX81 itself, its power supply and a vhf television set (black and white sets seem to work best). The ZX81 will happily work away without a tv attached, but you need to see what you are telling it to do, and it needs to tell you what it has done! Join up the three units as described in your manual. Turn on the power, switch on and then tune the tv. When correctly tuned (Channel 2 on the tuning knob), you see a white K in a black square at the bottom left — we call this the [K] cursor.

THE ZX81 KEYBOARD

It's worth-while taking trouble to get used to your ZX81 keyboard — it's been carefully designed to make each key do as much work as possible. These are the various items that the keys will produce on the screen:

(1) The set of keywords
These are the words in small white print above each letter key — they are the instructions which tell the ZX81 what to do. When the [K] cursor is showing and you press a letter key, you put the corresponding keyword on the screen — try any *one* now. I just pressed Y, which put the keyword **RETURN** on the screen and changed the [K] cursor to [L]. Some of you are asking the obvious question — "How do I choose between a letter and a keyword?" The answer is simple — you don't!

The ZX81 knows when keywords or letters are needed, and puts the correct cursor on the screen as required.

It's a help to remember that many keywords are placed above or near their initial letter, to help you to find them quickly. In this book, as in your manual, all words produced by a single keystroke are printed in bold type, for example:

PRINT **ABS** **TO**

(2) The set of letters
You can type any letter on the screen (or space or full stop) by pressing the corresponding key while the [K] cursor is showing. Try some now, and notice how the [L] moves ahead of your typing all the time. The next character you type is always printed at the current position of the cursor.

(3) The set of numbers
You can type these just like letters, except that numbers are printed regardless of whether the [K] or [L] cursor is showing, and they don't change the cursor from [K] to [L]. Notice the zero, Ø, which must not be confused with letter O. Be careful also with number 1 and letter I.

(4) The set of upper case characters
If you hold down **SHIFT** (bottom left on the keyboard) and press almost any letter or number key, you will print one of a whole collection of words, punctuation marks, and math symbols, printed in red on the top part of each key. The exceptions are **SHIFT** 1 and **SHIFT** 5 to 0 which print nothing on the screen — we'll see what they do later.

Five of the upper-case characters (**STOP, LPRINT, SLOW, FAST, LLIST**) are keywords for use with the [K] cursor, the rest for the [L] cursor only.

(5) The set of functions
These are printed in small white letters underneath each letter key. Hold down **SHIFT** while the [L] cursor is showing and press the key **FUNCTION/ENTER** on the far right. You will see the cursor change from [L] to [F], and if you now press any letter key (other than V) you will put the corresponding function on the screen. Functions are usually needed one at a time, so the cursor automatically changes back to [L].

(6) The set of graphics characters
Press the **GRAPHICS** key (**SHIFT** 9) while the [L] cursor is showing, and you will see the cursor change to [G] (it will stay like that until you press **GRAPHICS** again). Now you can experiment with a whole lot of special effects.

Press any letter or number key, and you will get its *inverse* (white on black), useful for emphasis. Hold down **SHIFT**, and press one of the block of 20 keys on the left of the keyboard, and you will get one of the special black/white/gray graphics blocks. Later on we'll be using these for drawing pictures and graphs. **SHIFT** with any other key will give you the inverse of the corresponding upper case character.

Now we know how to type any of the characters on the screen, so we can go on to write a program, but first we must clear the screen of rubbish. A quick way is to press **EDIT** (**SHIFT** 1), which empties the screen, leaving the [K] cursor. We get the same effect by unplugging the power jack plug, but remember for the future that this loses all the programs and data in the ZX81 — it's a last resort!

WE LEARNED THESE IN CHAPTER 4

Setting up the ZX81.
Sets of characters available from the keyboard.

Chapter 5

Your First Program

CLEARING OUT OLD PROGRAMS

You must get rid of any old programs from the ZX81 memory before you type in a new one. Right, I know there's nothing there, but let's practice anyway. At the end of the last chapter we set the cursor to [K], so all we have to do is to press key A and the keyword **NEW** appears on the screen. Now we need to pass this to the ZX81 for action, so we press **ENTER** on the far right of the keyboard. **NEW** vanishes from the screen — the ZX81 has now obeyed the command "clear out any old program and get ready for a new one" — and [K] reappears.

COMMANDS AND STATEMENTS

"When I use a word," said Humpty Dumpty, "it means just what I choose it to mean." We just used the instructions **NEW** and **ENTER**, and I am calling these *commands.* Commands are not part of a program, they are orders from outside the program that are obeyed once and then forgotten. Nearly all the keywords, plus upper case **EDIT, LPRINT, SLOW, FAST,** and **LLIST**, are accepted as commands by the ZX81. **INPUT** gives an error, and **FOR, NEXT, PAUSE, SCROLL** are not useful.

Statements, on the other hand, are instructions included in numbered program lines that form part of a program. They are remembered by the ZX81 and obeyed every time the program is run. Any keyword (except **CONT**) can be used as a statement, as well as upper case **STOP, LPRINT, SLOW, FAST, LLIST**.

WRITING A PROGRAM

And about time! We saw in Chapter 3 that all BASIC program lines must be numbered, so type a line number, say "1Ø". The cursor is still [K], because the first item after a line number *must* be a keyword, so now press key "P". You now have:

1Ø **PRINT** [L]

---

on the screen, so continue by typing:

1Ø **PRINT** "RULE 1 IN BASIC [L]

---

and then press **ENTER** to enter it into the ZX81 memory. What happened? Yes, yet another cursor [S] appeared! This marks a *syntax error,* something wrong with the line which prevents it from being entered. At the moment it is saying, "Quotes come in pairs!" so add the missing quote at the end and press **ENTER** again. This time your line 1Ø pops up to the top of the screen, it has gone into memory, and the [K] cursor reappears at the bottom, ready for the next program line.

No more lines for the present, we'll run the program as it stands. Press "R" to put the command **RUN** on the screen, and you know by now that the next key to press is **ENTER**.

When the cheering has died down, look carefully at what happened. The words and spaces inside your quotes have all been printed according to plan, while the line number, cursors, and quotes have been left out — they were there to tell the ZX81 what to do. What we did in line 1Ø was to **PRINT** a *literal string* on the screen. Literal strings are enclosed by quotes, and may contain *anything* from the keyboard except a **SHIFT** P quote (use **SHIFT** Q for a picture of a quote if you need one). At the bottom of the screen is Ø/1Ø, the ZX81's *report code,* which is saying "Program ran without problems and ended with line 1Ø." Your numbered program line is still in memory, where it will stay till you clear it out, or type **NEW,** or switch off. You can see it again if you wish by pressing **ENTER**.

Hidden under the report code is a [K] cursor, ready for your next program line. Let's go on to the next chapter and type some more.

WE LEARNED THESE IN CHAPTER 5

COMMANDS

NEW to clear out old programs.

ENTER to pass commands to the ZX81 and to enter numbered lines into a program.

RUN to make the ZX81 run your programs and carry out the instructions in them.

STATEMENTS

PRINT to print literal strings on the screen.

ANYTHING ELSE

Commands and statements.
The cursors.
Syntax errors.
Report codes.

CHAPTER 6

Tidy up Your Programs!

A SECOND LINE

Press **ENTER** if necessary to display the current program at the top of the screen, then type this second line exactly as printed:

---

20 **PRINT** "EVERY LINE NEEDS A NUMBERS" [L]

Sorry — some bad spelling there! Don't panic, hold down **SHIFT** and press **DELETE** twice. You will see the [L] cursor move back two spaces, rubbing out the quote and the offending S. Now retype the quote and press **ENTER**,, sending line 20 up to join the rest of the program. Run the program as before, and you'll get this on the screen:

```
RULE 1 IN BASIC
EVERY LINE NEEDS A NUMBER
```

plus the usual report code 0/20.
So far I've carefully printed in the cursor wherever it occurred in a program line. Now I'll leave it out unless there is a special reason.

TIDYING UP

The result will look neater if we put a space between the two lines of output. Try this — type:

```
15 PRINT
```

and enter it by pressing **ENTER**. What on earth are we trying to do? **PRINT** what? Well, run the program and see what happens. It worked, didn't it! When the ZX81 comes to a **PRINT** statement it prints what it is told to. In line 15 it was told to print nothing — nothing was what it printed!

Finally we'll add a comment to say what the program is about. Type the following:

```
5 REM ** MY FIRST PROGRAM
```

The **REM** statement is saying, "Ignore the rest of this line, it is only a programmer's remark." The ** are simply added to make the **REM** lines show up better.

NUMBERING AND LISTING

Most computers have to be asked for a list of lines in a program, but ZX81 gives you a list as soon as you press **ENTER** or when you add a line to your program. I'm sure you've noticed that the ZX81 has sorted the lines into numerical order, although we typed 10, 20, 15, 5. I expect you have also realized why we left gaps between the line numbers. Yes, it makes it easy to insert lines later on, as we did with lines 15 and 5. ZX81 does not care what the line numbers are, it is only interested in the *order*. There is a choice of line numbers from 1 to 9999, so there's no shortage.

GETTING RID OF WHOLE PROGRAM LINES

Let's suppose we want to erase line 5 to save memory space — often the ultimate fate of **REM** lines. Simply type the line number 5 and press **ENTER**. Line 5 has gone, just like that! Alternatively you can completely change a line by typing its line number, then the new version, and then pressing **ENTER**. You can do this as often as you like, ZX81 will always delete an old line and replace it with the new one.

Now for a couple of exercises to practice what we have learned in the last two chapters.

EXERCISE 6.1. LINE CHANGING

Delete lines 15 and 2Ø of the current program, then change line 1Ø to make the ZX81 print the message:

THREE LINES GONE, ONE LEFT

EXERCISE 6.2. YOUR ADDRESS

Delete the old program with a single keyword (remember which one?). Write a program to print your name and address as though on an envelope. Just to show it can be done, leave gaps of 1ØØØ between your line numbers.

WE LEARNED THESE IN CHAPTER 6

STATEMENTS

PRINT to make a line space.
REM for a remark, ignored by the ZX81.

ANYTHING ELSE

DELETE to delete characters one at a time in a line you are writing.
Automatic listing by pressing **ENTER.**
Line numbering with gaps for later additions.
Deleting and changing existing lines.

CHAPTER 7

Sums? No Problem!

Until now I have been reminding you to press **ENTER** to pass commands and program lines from the bottom of the screen to the ZX81. From now on it's up to you!

KEYWORDS IN COMMAND MODE

We have used **PRINT** as a statement in program lines, but we saw in Chapter 5 that most keywords could also be used as commands. Try typing:

PRINT "THIS IS A ONE-OFF COMMAND"

The ZX81 obeys the command *once,* but it is then forgotten and cannot be obeyed again. The report code Ø/Ø shows that there was no line number.

NUMBERS AND EXPRESSIONS

We can make the ZX81 print *numbers* in the same way as we have printed strings, except that quotes must not be used. Try a few like:

PRINT 99
PRINT Ø.Ø75
PRINT 3.74
PRINT .625

The full stop doubles as a decimal point, and leading 0s on the left of the decimal point need not be included.

Expressions consist of numbers and operators, for example 5 + 3. If we ask the ZX81 to print an expression, it will helpfully work out the answer and print that. Type in:

PRINT 5 + 3

The answer 8 appears at the top of the screen — we have used the ZX81 like a pocket calculator, but with the advantage that we can see the whole expression, and if necessary correct it, before it is worked out.

OPERATORS AND PRIORITY

We all remember the four standard math operators. You will find – and + easily at **SHIFT** J and **SHIFT** K. Instead of × or "multiplied by" we use * (**SHIFT** B), and for ÷ or "divided by" we use / (**SHIFT** V) — this is standard computer practice. In addition, we have ** (**SHIFT** H) which means "raised to the power of":

2**3 = 2^3 = 2 × 2 × 2 = 8

Try typing more simple expressions, each made of a pair of numbers with an operator:

PRINT 25 – 17 **PRINT** 7 – 12 **PRINT** 9*11
PRINT 63/9 **PRINT** 125/48

Notice that the ZX81 copes with negative numbers and decimals. If you type:

PRINT 2/3 and **PRINT** 1/3

you will find the answer printed to 8 decimal places, the last place being rounded up or down as usual.

What happens with longer expressions like:

2 + 3*4?

If we are doing sums like these on paper, we have to follow a standard *order of operations.* ZX81 and most computers do the same.

Highest priority	**	(to the power of)
⇩	* and /	(times and divided by)
Lowest priority	+ and –	(plus and minus)

So the expression above is worked out in two stages:

(1) 3 * 4 = 12
(2) 2 + 12 = 14 (answer)

Try these expressions, and make up more of your own:

PRINT 7*2 – 5	**PRINT** 9 – 12/6
PRINT 3**3 + 5	**PRINT** 38 – 5**2

Make sure you are getting the answers you expect!

USING PARENTHESES

If we want to tell the ZX81 to *change* its priority rules, we can do so by using parentheses. The ZX81 will follow standard mathematical rules and work out the part of the expression inside parentheses first. Compare these two expressions:

PRINT	2 + 3 * 4	**PRINT**	(2 + 3) * 4
(1)	3 × 4 = 12	(1)	2 + 3 = 5
(2)	2 + 12 = 14	(2)	5 × 4 = 20

Check that the ZX81 gives the right answers. You can use as many parentheses as you like, *in pairs,* either separately or nested inside each other. When the ZX81 meets nested parentheses, it starts with the expression in the inside pair(s) and then works it way outwards. Don't hesitate to use extra (unnecessary) pairs of parentheses if it makes an expression easier for *you* to understand.

EXERCISE 7.1. EXPRESSIONS WITH PARENTHESES

Work out the answers to these expressions, then check them with the ZX81.

```
((7 - 5)*(30/12))**3
(((6*8) - (23 - 11))/(5 + 7))**2
```

SCIENTIFIC NOTATION

Type these commands and look carefully at the answers:

```
PRINT .ØØØØ7
PRINT 7/1Ø**5
PRINT 7ØØØØØØØØØØØØØ (12 Øs)
PRINT 7*1Ø**12
```

and now these:

```
PRINT .ØØØØØ7
PRINT 7/1Ø**6
PRINT 7ØØØØØØØØØØØØØØ (13 Øs)
PRINT 7*1Ø**13
```

When numbers get too big or too small, ZX81 prints them in scientific notation:

7E + 13 is the same as 7*10**13 or 7×10^{13}
7E − 6 is the same as 7/10**6 or $7/10^{6}$ or 7×10^{-6}

Many calculators use just the same method to accommodate small and large numbers.

If we wish, we can use scientific notation for the numbers we pass to the ZX81. Type:

```
PRINT 7E - 5
PRINT 7E - 6
```

and so on. The ZX81 always changes to normal decimal notation if it has room.

WE LEARNED THESE IN CHAPTER 7

COMMANDS

PRINT to print strings, numbers or the answers to expressions.

ANYTHING ELSE

Mathematical operators and priority.
Parentheses to change priority.
Scientific notation.

CHAPTER 8
Vital Variables

We have seen how to command the ZX81 to print numbers, or the answers to expressions, on the screen. We can do the same in a program, but is not particularly useful, and we have a far more powerful statement available, **LET.**

DEFINING A VARIABLE WITH LET

Clear the ZX81 with **NEW,** and then type this line:

```
10 LET X = 5
```

Run it — there's no output apart form the 0/10 "O.K." message — what have we done this time? Well, in long-winded English we have said, "Label a memory box X and put 5 in it." In other words we have defined the variable X as having the value 5.

Now we can do all sorts of things with the contents of X. We can print it:

```
20 PRINT X (and RUN)
```

We can use it in expressions:

```
30 PRINT 100*X
40 PRINT X**3
```

Note that, although we have used the contents of box X in lines 20, 30, 40, the 5 is still there. Check this by adding:

```
50 PRINT X
```

The original 5 *is* still there, but we *can* change it if we wish.

```
60 LET X = 999
70 PRINT X
```

Line 60 said, "Throw out the contents of box X and insert 999." We can change the value of a variable as often as we like — that's why it's called a variable.

NAMING VARIABLES

The number of variables we can use in a program is limited only by memory space, but they must all have different names! ZX81 offers the widest choice of names in town, you just have to follow these rules:

(1) Variable names *must* start with a letter, not a number.
(2) Variable names *may* contain any mixture of letters and numbers, but not spaces (ignored) or any other characters (illegal).

We generally use short names to save memory and effort, often choosing mnemonics (memory joggers) of the contents — T for total, W for weight, and so on. Try out your own names for variables, using **LET** as a command if you wish, and see what happens when you break the rules above.

MORE ADVANCED LET STATEMENTS

Our statement has the general form:

LET variable name = . . .

What can we put on the right of the = sign? Here are some examples, the first we have seen already.

(1) A number:
LET B = 75

(2) An expression using numbers:
LET C = 23*45

(3) An expression using other variables, with or without numbers:
LET A = C   **LET** V = B**3
Important — you can only put a variable on the right if it has already been defined. ZX81 refuses to work with variables it does not know about.

(4) An expression using the same variable as the one on the left:
LET B = B + 1Ø   **LET** A = A*X
Algebra was never like this! Remember that these are not equations. We are saying things like, "Take out the contents of box B, add 10 to it and put this new value back into box B."

HOW WE USE VARIABLES

If we know the radius (R) of a circle, we can use these well known equations to work out the diameter (D), circumference (C), and area (A).

$D = 2R$
$C = \pi D$
$A = \pi R^2$

(let's take π as 3.14 for now).

We can put all this into a simple program. First we define R, the radius of the circle in inches (in) or centimeters (cm):

```
10 LET R = 5
```

Next we calculate the three unknowns and use them to define variables.

```
20 LET D = 2*R
30 LET C = 3.14*D
40 LET A = R**2*3.14
```

Finally we can print the results:

```
50 PRINT R
60 PRINT D
70 PRINT C
80 PRINT A
```

Run the program and check the results with a pocket calculator. We can make the results less anonymous by printing titles:

```
45 PRINT "RADIUS GIVEN="
55 PRINT "DIAMETER="
65 PRINT "CIRCUMFERENCE="
75 PRINT "AREA="
```

You can change to any other given radius by rewriting line 10. Not a bad little program, but what a messy printout! We'll tidy it up in the next chapter.

EXERCISE 8.1. MONEY CHANGING

Today's exchange rate is U.S.A. $1.90 for a British £1. Write a program to print out the number of $ you must have for £75, and how many £ you will get for $250.

EXERCISE 8.2. PARACHUTING

One of the Golden Knights parachute team jumps from his plane at 3000 meters. The distance he drops (S) is given by $S = AT^2/2$ where A is the acceleration due to gravity = 9.8 m/s/s and T is the time in seconds after jumping (air resistance ignored). Write a program to calculate his height after 10 seconds. If he must pull the rip cord 500 meters above the ground, use your program to find roughly how many seconds his free fall will last.

WE LEARNED THESE IN CHAPTER 8

STATEMENTS

LET to define a variable.
PRINT to print the current value of a variable.

ANYTHING ELSE

Rules for naming variables.
Various ways of using variables.

CHAPTER 9

A Little Punctuation Works Wonders

So far we have been using **PRINT** to print items on successive lines of the screen. We often want to put several items on the same line — try this short program:

```
10 PRINT "AREA OF A SQUARE"
20 PRINT
30 LET S=4
40 PRINT "SIDE= "; S; "CM"
```

Run it, and look carefully at the result of line 40. The vital parts are the semicolons which are saying, "Don't move to a new line, print the next item immediately after this". You can use semicolons as here, in between **PRINT** items on a line, or you can put one at the end of a **PRINT** line — the next **PRINT** item will always be printed right after the last. Notice that we wanted a space between S and CM, so we had to include one inside the quotes.

Now change the program like this:

```
35 LET A=S*S
40 PRI "SIDE="; S; "CM", "AREA="; A; "SQ CM"
```

Another useful bit of punctuation is the comma. Each line is divided into two halves, and the comma says, "Move to the beginning of the next half and print the next item there." You can use commas in clusters if you like, each one moves the print position to the beginning of the next half line.

We already know that full stop has the function of a decimal point. Apart from this, the rest of the punctuation (. : ?) can be used in literal strings but has no other special use.

TABULATION

How many characters can you pack into one line of the screen? Try this:

```
20 PRINT "01234567890123 4 . . .
```

After a while your numbers run onto the next line, but remember that your 2Ø **PRINT** " takes up some space. Stop typing numbers when the [L] is exactly beneath the first Ø, add your final quotes and press **ENTER**. Now if you run the program, you will get a complete line of 32 numbers (to check up, type another line with one more number). We can complete the line numbering by printing the tens, starting with ten spaces:

```
10 PRINT "1111111111222222222233"
```

Now check the comma print position by typing:

```
30 PRINT
40 PRINT "FIRST HALF", "SECOND HALF"
```

Now change and extend your program like this (remember that **TAB** is one of the set of functions):

```
40 PRINT "ONE"
50 PRINT TAB 7; "TWO"
60 PRINT TAB 15; "BUCKLE"
70 PRINT TAB 23; "MY SHOE"
```

It's pretty obvious what's happening. **TAB** n; moves the print position to number n and the next item is printed there. You must follow **TAB** n with ; (, is possible but not usually sensible).

You often need to print several **TAB** items on the same line. No trouble — simply put in more semicolons to stop the ZX81 moving to the next line. Here is a bank statement heading, to replace your nursery rhyme:

```
40 PRINT TAB 8;"BANK STATEMENT"
50 PRINT
60 PRINT
70 PRINT "DATE"; TAB 6; "DEBIT"; TAB 14; "CREDIT"; TAB 24;
   "BALANCE"
```

We can print numbers, expressions or variables at **TAB** positions, in just the same way as we have printed literal strings. Here are some more advanced rules about **TAB** — they will come in useful later on.

(1) We do not need to use a number after **TAB**, we can use a variable (previously defined), or an expression containing numbers and variables.
(2) If the number after **TAB** is a decimal, it will be rounded to the nearest whole number (7.5 rounded to 8).
(3) If the number after **TAB** is more than 31, it will be divided by 32 and the remainder used as the **TAB** number.

EXERCISE 9.1. CIRCLES

Now go back to Chapter 8 and retype the last program there to give a printout like this:

```
VITAL STATISTICS OF A CIRCLE
IF THE RADIUS IS 5 IN
DIAM = 10 IN CIRCUMF = 31.4 IN
AREA = 78.5 SQ IN
```

When you have written the program, keep it to use in the next chapter.

WE LEARNED THESE IN CHAPTER 9

; , and **TAB** to vary the **PRINT** position on a line of the screen.

CHAPTER 10

Anyone Can Make a Mistake!

So far we have seen two ways of correcting mistakes in a program. You can use **DELETE** in the line you are currently typing, or you can delete or replace an existing line by typing its line number plus the new version.

If we need to change a long line already entered into the program, the first method will not work, and the second takes a long time. The answer is to **EDIT** the line.

THE CURRENT LINE POINTER

Let's look at our program first. I am going to edit my version of the Circles program (Exercise 9.1 in Chapter 9). You could type my answer out yourself, or try editing your own version.

If you look at the program on the screen, you will find that one of the line numbers has a cursor > beside it — the current line pointer or program cursor. Unless you have moved it, it will be at the last line you typed in. The first job is to move the current line pointer to the line you want to edit:

(1) If it has not far to move, you can use ⇧(**SHIFT** 7) or ⇩(**SHIFT** 6) to push it up or down, line by line.
(2) To move it to the beginning of the program, type **LIST** and

ENTER. The pointer, apparently vanished, has gone to an imaginary line Ø, and can be brought down with ⇩ .

(3) To move it anywhere else, type **LIST** line number. Part of the program will be displayed, starting at that line number, with the point right there.

Practice moving your pointer up and down your program, using these three methods.

EDITING A LINE

I want to edit my current line 9Ø:

```
9Ø PRINT "DIAM = "; D;" IN", "CIRCUMF = "; C;" IN"
```

by deleting all reference to diameter, and printing circumference in full at **TAB** 3.

First I put the current line pointer on line 9Ø and press **EDIT** (**SHIFT** 1). Line 9Ø is immediately printed in full at the bottom of the screen, with the [K] cursor following the number 9Ø. Now I can move the [K] cursor backwards or forwards along the line using ⇦ (**SHIFT** 5) or ⇨ (**SHIFT** 8), without changing the contents of the line. Try it, press ⇨ repeatedly and see the cursor skip along the line, changing to [L] as it passes **PRINT**. Stop it when it has just passed the comma in the middle of the line, then use **DELETE** to remove everything back to the first quote. You now have:

```
9Ø PRINT [L] "CIRCUMF = ";C;" IN"
```

Type in **TAB** 3 and then move the cursor along to just after CIRCUMF and type in the missing ERENCE.

If you mess up your editing, you can always press **EDIT** again and bring down the original version of the line.

Assuming that you are happy with the edited version:

```
9Ø PRINT TAB 3;"CIRCUMFERENCE = ";C;" IN"
```

press **ENTER**, and it immediately appears in its right place in the program, the old version disappearing forever.

RENUMBERING LINES

We'll renumber line 9Ø and make it line 1Ø5 — no trouble with the ZX81. Press **EDIT** to bring the line down for editing, and then press **DELETE** twice to remove the 9Ø. Type in the new number 1Ø5 and press **ENTER** to put line 1Ø5 into the program. Old line 9Ø is still there — you'll have to type 9Ø **ENTER** to get rid of this.

SOME FINAL POINTS

Remember that you can also use the arrows to edit a line you are writing for the first time.

If you write a long program, you will not be able to see the whole thing on the screen. The ZX81 will do its best to show you the bit you are currently working on. Otherwise you can type **LIST** n to display line n plus as many following lines as there is room for.

When your ZX81 memory is nearly full, you will find that **EDIT** has no effect, especially with long program lines. The remedy is to type **CLS** and **ENTER**. This clears the screen and **EDIT** will now bring the current line down for editing.

WE LEARNED THESE IN CHAPTER 10

COMMANDS

EDIT to change a line which has already been entered in your program.
LIST, LIST n to see different parts of a long program.

ANYTHING ELSE

The current line pointer and how to move it up and down.
How to move the line cursor.
Renumbering lines.

CHAPTER 11

Strictly Functional

The functions are all to be seen under the letter keys — together with a few oddments that are not functions. Don't worry if you don't recognize some of the math functions in this chapter, just move on to the useful number-chopping functions at the end.

A function of a number is an instruction to carry out some operation on that number and produce the answer. The number to be operated on — it can equally well be an expression or a variable — is sometimes called the "argument" of the function. Try typing these commands:

PRINT SQR 81
LET A = 25 and then **PRINT SQR** A
PRINT SQR 2
PRINT SQR (A*9)

I expect you have recognized *SQR* as your old friend the square root — a number that when multiplied by itself gives the number you started with. Notice that in the last example we wanted the square root of an *expression,* so we had to put the expression in parentheses. A function always operates on the numbers or variable immediately following it, unless there are parentheses to tell it otherwise. Put another way, a function has a *higher priority* than any of the math operators.

We can use more than one function together — in this case these functions are carried out one by one from right to left. For example:

PRINT LN SQR 16

gives us the natural logarithm (to base e) of the square root of 16. We only have natural logs available on ZX81, by the way, with natural antilog alongside (**EXP** or e^x).

THE TRIG FUNCTIONS

Take any circle, divide the circumference by the diameter, and you get a constant a little over 3 which we call PI (Greek letter π). For a more accurate version type:

PRINT PI (π on the keyboard)

The trig functions are all functions of angles, and ZX81 needs the angles to be expressed in *radians*. We can easily convert degrees to radians, remembering that:

PI radians = 180°

Try this little trig table program, if you are interested:

```
10 LET XD = 30
20 REM XD IS ANGLE IN DEGREES
30 LET XR = XD*PI/180
40 REM XR IS NOW IN RADIANS
50 PRINT XD;" DEGREES",XR;" RADIANS"
60 PRINT,, "SIN = "; SIN XR
70 PRINT,, "COS="; COS XR
80 PRINT,, "TAN="; TAN XR
```

(note ,, for line spaces in 60, 70, 80).

Run the program, and try inserting different angles in line 10 — check the results in a book of trig tables. Jot down a set of results, for example:

60° SIN = 0.8660254 COS = 0.5
TAN = 1.7320508

Now type the command:

```
PRINT ASN Ø.866Ø254*18Ø/PI
```

and you are back with your original angle of 60°. **ASN** X (ARCSIN on the keyboard) gives you "the angle in radians whose SIN is X." ARCCOS and ARCTAN do the same for COS and TAN.

HERE COMES A CHOPPER

More functions — **INT, ABS**, and **SGN** — let's learn by doing:

```
 1Ø LET N = 3
1ØØ PRINT "NUMBER"; TAB 8; "INT", "ABS"; TAB 24; "SGN"
11Ø PRINT
12Ø PRINT N; TAB 8; INT N, ABS N; TAB 24; SGN N
```

Put all sorts of numbers into N in line 1Ø — whole numbers, decimal numbers, negative numbers. In case you are feeling lazy, here are some examples:

NO.	*INT*	*ABS*	*SGN*
3	3	3	1
3.14	3	3.14	1
0.14	0	0.14	1
0	0	0	0
−3	−3	3	−1
−3.14	−4	3.14	−1

It's pretty obvious what **INT** is doing (especially if you graduated on a Sinclair ZX80). **INT** chops off and loses the decimal part of a number, leaving the nearest integer (or whole number) which is less than the original number.

3.14 gives (the nearest integer less than 3.14)
−3.14 gives −4 (the nearest integer less than −3.14)

ABS is another chopper — this time it removes any negative signs and replaces them with positive signs, in other words **ABS** gives the absolute value of N.

Wield the axe once more with **SGN**. This time the entire number has gone, and we are left with nothing but its sign, + or −, attached to a 1.0 has no sign, so **SGN** 0 = 0.

EXERCISE 11.1. DECIMAL PART

There's no function to produce the decimal part of a number — it's up to you. Write a program to print a number and then its integer and decimal parts in three columns.

ROUNDING-OFF NUMBERS

Computers often produce an embarrassing number of decimal places, so *rounding-off* is a valuable operation. **INT** will not do this on its own — to see why, type:

PRINT INT 7.Ø1 and **PRINT INT** 7.99

Both give 7, which is obviously unfair to 7.99, which is so very nearly 8. The answer is to add 0.5 to the number before we apply **INT** — this is how it works:

N	N + 0.5	INT (N + 0.5)
7.01	7.51	7
7.49	7.99	7
7.5	8.0	8
7.99	8.49	8

EXERCISE 11.2

We've seen how to round numbers to the nearest whole number. Write a program line to round a number to one decimal place. Hint — multiply by 10 first, round the result to the nearest whole number, then divide by 10. Try it now.

I hope you managed that one all right. In the same way, you can round to any number of decimal places, or to the nearest ten, hundred, and so on.

There's one more important point. ZX81 needs *integers* to follow certain statements. We have met **TAB** n and **LIST** n already, and there are these others:

PLOT	**UNPLOT**	**RUN**	**DIM**	**GOTO**
GOSUB	**PAUSE**	**PRINT**	**AT**	**PRINT (TO)**

You are also allowed to use variables or expressions with these statements — the ZX81 will work out the values for you. The trouble here is that expressions and variables often deliver decimal numbers. Don't worry! ZX81 will also round the values up or down to the nearest integer, just like we did at the beginning of this section.

WE LEARNED THESE IN CHAPTER 11

Functions — math, trig, **INT, ABS**, and **SGN**.
Rounding-off numbers.
Automatic rounding-off by ZX81, when integers are required following statements (**LIST** n and so on).

CHAPTER 12

Magic Roundabout

Do you remember *The Sorcerer's Apprentice* in Chapter 3? Here is a mathematical model of a broom filling a 150 gallon water tank at the rate of 4 gallons per trip. We need to make room for a lot of trips, so I am introducing a new statement, **SCROLL**. This moves the contents of the screen one line up, making room for the next item which is printed on the bottom line (like rolling up a scroll!). At this stage the screen is technically full, so to print something else we have to **SCROLL** again. Type in this program:

```
10 LET W = 0
20 LET W = W + 4
30 SCROLL
40 PRINT W; "GALLONS"
50 GOTO 20
```

Line 10 empties the tank at the start.
Line 20 puts 4 gallons of water in the tank.
Lines 30, 40 print the total water added to the tank so far.
Line 50 contains a really important new statement — **GOTO** 20 means, "Go straight to line 20 and continue running the program from there." In other words, "Take a trip to the well for more water."

Can you predict the result of this program? Run it and see . . . . . . water, water, everywhere! How can we stop the onward march of the brooms? **BREAK** (bottom right of keyboard, no **SHIFT** needed) is the emergency button, it will always stop the ZX81 while it is working, so press it now. You can restart after **BREAK** by pressing **CONT**, though your screen contents will be lost.

Well, we made a *loop* around lines 2Ø to 5Ø — **GOTO** is certainly an easy way to get lots of output! In Chapter 3, we saw that we need to include a *conditional jump* in the loop to check whether the tank is full, we'll do that now. Change line 5Ø and add two more lines:

```
5Ø IF W < 15Ø THEN GOTO 2Ø
6Ø SCROLL
7Ø PRINT "TANK FILLED. WHAT NOW?"
```

There, that worked pretty well, didn't it (apart from a small spill of 2 gallons). Line 5Ø contains the most important bit of programming so far. It is saying, "Check the value of W, if less than 150 then go back to line 2Ø, if it's 150 or more go on to the next line." BASIC wastes no words!

RELATIONAL OPERATORS

Line 5Ø has the general form:

IF something is true **THEN** do something
e.g., W < 15Ø e.g., **GOTO** 2Ø

The **IF** keyword is always followed by a statement using one of the *relational operators* which are used to *compare* two items:

=	equals
<	is less than
>	is greater than
<=	is less than or equal to
>=	is greater than or equal to
<>	is not equal to

On either side of these operators, we put the two items being compared, which may consist of numbers, variables, or expressions:

IF A = 100 **THEN**. . .
IF B < 0 **THEN** . . .
IF C > A + 21 **THEN** . . .
IF D <> A + B **THEN** . . .

and so on.

IF SOMETHING IS TRUE THEN WHAT?

The program above used:

. . . **THEN GOTO** 20

which is a very common form of conditional statement. However, **THEN** produces the keyword cursor [K] (did you notice?), and it can be followed by any of the keywords, though some don't make much sense. Common ones are:

GOTO **PRINT** **LET**
GOSUB **RETURN** (we'll meet these later)

Here are some examples of lines with conditional statements:

```
100 IF X > 21 THEN PRINT "OVER 21 AND BUST"
200 IF T > = Z THEN GOTO 1000
300 IF P < 0 THEN LET P = 0
```

GOTO WHERE?

Whether **GOTO** is compulsory or conditional, it must be followed by a line number. In that way, you direct the ZX81 to any line in your program, either before or after the **GOTO** line. We can use a line number as such, or we can use a variable or an expression (all variables defined, of course). If the result is a decimal number, the ZX81 will round it off to an integer, and if the line number is nonexistent the ZX81 will go to the next line which does exist.

HOW ABOUT STOP?

With all this to-ing and fro-ing, it's as well to know how to stop! Try this program:

```
100 LET S = 78
200 IF S > 100 THEN GOTO 400
300 PRINT "YOU LOST. SCORE = "; S
400 PRINT "WINNER. SCORE 100 +"
```

If you run it, you'll see that you need something to stop the ZX81 from charging on and doing both the orders in lines 300 and 400.

```
350 STOP
```

Add this and all is well. Try the program with different values of S, and make sure it works.

Now here are two problems for you, each needing loops with **IF . . . THEN** statements.

EXERCISE 12.1. BUILDING INTEREST ON SAVINGS

The savings and loan office offers you 8% compound interest calculated annually. If you deposit $500 in 1982 and leave it to grow, after one year you have:

$$500 \times \frac{108}{100} = \$540$$

After two years:

$$540 \times \frac{108}{100} \text{ and so on.}$$

Write a program to show how your savings build up over seven years, finishing in 1989. Then change one line to round off each result to the nearest penny (see Chapter 11).

EXERCISE 12.2. WHEN ARE THE LEAP YEARS?

The test for a leap year is "are the last two digits divisible by 4?" Write a program to print out the years from 1982 to 1999, and say which are leap years. The table below will help:

Year Y	Year divided by 4 Y/4	*INT* (Y/4)	Is *INT* (Y/4) equal to Y/4?
1982	20.5	20	NO
1984	21	21	YES

WE LEARNED THESE IN CHAPTER 12

COMMANDS

BREAK to stop the ZX81 while it is working.
CONT to restart after **BREAK**.

STATEMENTS

SCROLL to move the screen contents up one line so that the next item is printed at the bottom of the screen.
GOTO n directs the ZX81 to line n of the program.
IF condition **THEN** statement, executes the statement (**GOTO**, etc.) if the condition (X < 10, etc.) is met.
STOP to stop a program and to avoid crashing into later program lines.

ANYTHING ELSE

Relational operators (=, <, >, <=, >=, <>) to compare two items.

CHAPTER 13
Flowcharts

We are able to write quite complicated programs, now that we have learned about loops and conditional branching. At this stage, it is worth reminding ourselves about *flowcharts* as an aid to good programming.

Suppose you have some operation for which you want to write a program — let's use the sorcerer's apprentice idea from Chapter 3 as an example. The idea of a flowchart is to split the operation up into separate stages, to write each stage in a box, and to join the boxes by arrows to show the order in which the stages have to be done. We use boxes of these shapes:

Beginning or end.

"Processing block" — one stage of the operation that needs no decision.

"Decision diamond" — here a question is asked and the flowchart branches to either side depending on the answer.

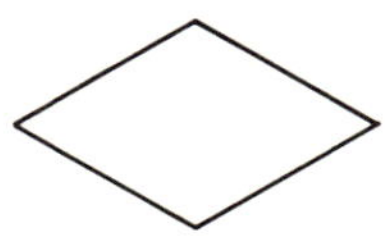

FLOWCHART FOR A PROGRAM

Now we can draw up a flowchart for filling the water tank from the well. Compare it with the original program in Chapter 3, and with the mathematical model in the last chapter. Notice how the place of the IF . . . THEN . . . statement is taken by the decision diamond.

Some people can carry a flowchart in their heads and type out a program direct. However, most of us will benefit from drawing up a flowchart on paper first. We'll see more examples of flowcharts for ZX81 programs later.

BROOM FILLING WATER TANK FROM WELL

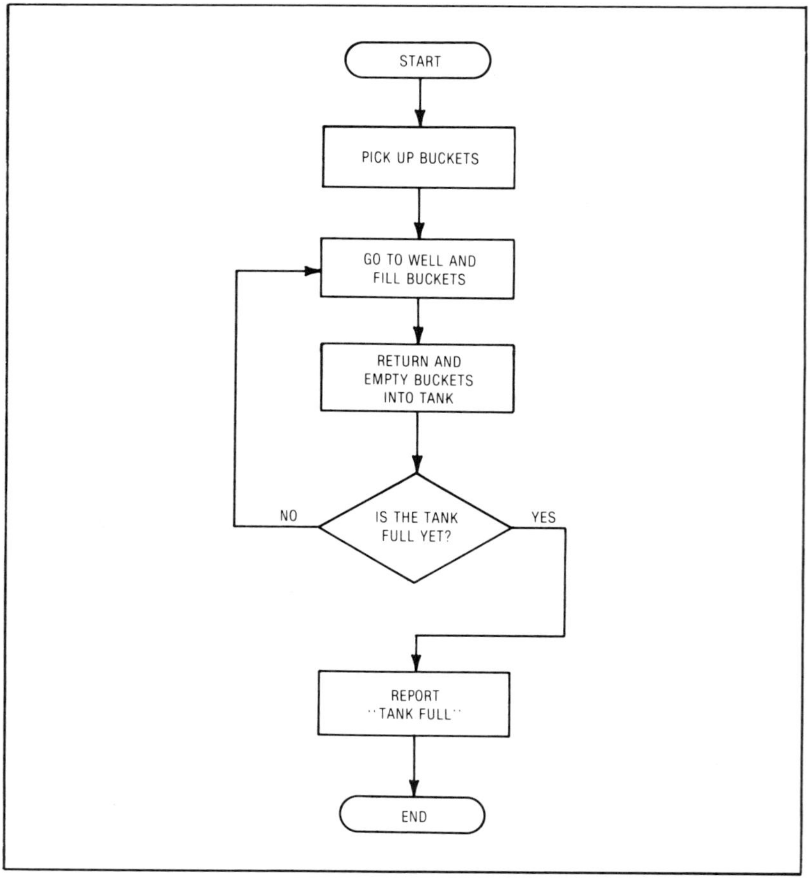

CHAPTER 14

Putting in Data

Let's go back to Exercise 12.1 in Chapter 12 — you'll find the listing in Appendix 4. Not a bad program, giving you interest at 8% a year for 7 years on your $500, but what a bore if you want to change your capital — you have to retype line 40. Well, we can do better than that. Type out the listing for Exercise 12.1, but change line 20 to read:

```
20 INPUT C
```

Run the program — what's this? A blank screen with an [L] cursor at the bottom! ZX81 is trying to say, "I've stopped and I'm waiting for you to put in a value for variable C." Type 500 and then press **ENTER** — you'll get just the same output as you got before with:

```
20 LET C = 500
```

but of course now you can make C different every time you run. Try running a few times and varying C. **INPUT** is great!

It makes things easier for people using your programs if you print a "prompt" to tell them what data they are supposed to be putting in. Add one more line:

```
10 PRINT "WHAT IS YOUR CAPITAL?"
```

Much easier to use now, isn't it? Stay with us, there's more to come.

INPUT LOOPS

After running the program, suppose you want it to go back to the beginning and run again with different capital. What instruction would you use? You guessed it:

```
150 GOTO 10
```

Type that in, and run it twice with different values for C.

Hmm . . . not so good, it crashed with a 5/100 report code. You can check that in your manual — it means "screen full", and we've got to do something about that next. We could use **SCROLL**, can you imagine your output rolling up the screen with a pause now and again for input. In this case, it's more elegant to wipe the screen before each new printout — the statement is **CLS** (clear screen). Here's the complete listing:

```
 10 PRINT,, "WHAT IS YOUR CAPITAL?"
 20 INPUT C
 30 CLS
 50 LET Y = 1982
100 PRINT Y;" CAPITAL + INTEREST = $";C
110 PRINT
120 LET Y = Y + 1
130 LET C = C*1.08
140 IF Y < 1990 THEN GOTO 100
150 GOTO 10
```

We now have two loops, one inside the other (nested). Why can't we put **CLS** at the beginning of the outside loop? Try it.

GETTING OUT OF AN INPUT LOOP

Well — it's not the most enthralling of programs, but how do you stop it, it seems capable of demanding data forever! The official way is to type **STOP** at the next pause for input, and then **ENTER** will stop the program with a D/20 message. If you happen to want to restart you type **CONT**, the ZX81 will still be at line 20 waiting for data, though **CONT** will have cleared the screen.

PERMANENT LOOPS

This input loop is a permanent loop, which is really only allowable because of the **INPUT** statement which stops it in line 20. If we change line 20 back to:

```
20 LET C = 500
```

we shall find that the poor old ZX81 goes round and round the outside loop indefinitely — or until we press **BREAK**. Some bad programming there!

Now for some examples for you to try, using **INPUT** loops:

EXERCISE 14.1. PERCENTAGES

Write a program to convert your exam results into percentages. You'll have to input your mark, the maximum possible mark, and then use

$$\frac{\text{Mark}}{\text{Max. mark}} \times 100 = \text{Mark\%}.$$

EXERCISE 14.2. GASOLINE CONSUMPTION

Write a program to input the number of miles driven, gallons used, and to calculate miles per gallon.

WE LEARNED THESE IN CHAPTER 14

STATEMENTS

INPUT to stop the program to enter values of variables.
CLS to clear the screen to make room for more output.
STOP as input to get out of an input loop.
CONT to restart after **STOP.**

ANYTHING ELSE

Input loops to stop repeatedly to collect data.

CHAPTER 15

Saving Programs and Data

USING THE ZX PRINTER

Imagine, you've written a program that works and you want to make a permanent record if it. When you switch the power off, the program will be lost and you'll have to work it out again. Obviously you can write it down on paper, but this is hard work and it's easy to make mistakes. It's very much easier if you happen to own a Sinclair ZX Printer, and you have had the forethought to plug it in before you started (Sinclair recommends that you do not connect the printer without switching the power off first). In this case, you can make a list on paper of all the lines of your program by typing the command **LLIST**. If you only want to record part of the program, you can type **LLIST** n to list from line number n onwards, and you can always press **BREAK** to stop printing whenever you like.

Another way of using your printer is to make a record on paper of any data that your program has worked out and printed on the tv screen. Use the keyword **COPY**, either as a command or a statement, to make the printer record the whole contents of the tv screen on paper.

BACKUP STORAGE

Whether you have copied the program by hand or with the ZX printer, you have a lot of typing to do when you want to use it again. You can save yourself all that typing by putting the program into *backup storage,* which for the ZX81 means almost any tape recorder.

THE ZX81 AND THE ZX PRINTER, DESIGNED ESPECIALLY FOR USE WITH SINCLAIR PERSONAL COMPUTERS

SAVING A PROGRAM

My cassette recorder has 3.5 mm jack plugs for microphone (MIC) and earpiece (EAR) and automatic recording level. It has a reliable tape counter (very useful), and a red LED indicator for recording level (a meter is just as good). If your own tape recorder lacks some of these features, you may have to adapt, and you will probably find it less convenient.

You'll need to keep a tape specially for ZX81 programs, with a careful record of its contents. Here is a list of operations that work for me — if you run into trouble you will find Chapter 16 in the ZX81 Manual very helpful.

(1) Connect the MIC sockets on ZX81 and recorder.
(2) Wind the tape back to the start, zero the counter, wind the tape to an empty stretch and note the counter reading.
(3) If you wish, record the name of the program on tape using your microphone (useful if you have no counter).

(4) Type the command **SAVE** "NAME" (your choice of name). Make a note of the name.
(5) Press the RECORD and PLAY keys on the tape recorder, then press **ENTER**. After a five-second blank, you will see a quickly changing set of thin black and white stripes (your program). Check that it is being recorded (LED or meter).
(6) At the end, the screen will go blank with a Ø/Ø report code. Switch off the tape recorder. Your program is still unchanged in the ZX81.

It's best to leave decent spaces — say five seconds — between the programs on your tape. A full 1K program takes about 15 to 20 seconds to record.

LOADING YOUR PROGRAM

Tomorrow has come — you want to put your program back into the ZX81. This is how I do it.

(1) Wind the tape to the point where recording started.
(2) Connect the EAR sockets on ZX81 and recorder.
(3) Type **LOAD** "NAME" or **LOAD**" ".
(4) Set the tape recorder volume to about ¾ of maximum, and any tone controls to maximum treble, minimum bass.
(5) Press **ENTER** — you will see various fairly even patterns on the screen, and then suddenly a rapidly moving pattern of horizontal bars, a bit like a venetian blind gone crazy. This is your program.
(6) After loading, the screen will clear with a Ø/Ø report code. Switch off the tape recorder.
(7) You can now press **ENTER** for a listing of the program, or **RUN** to run it.

IT'S BETTER TO LOAD A NAMED PROGRAM

One gets lazy and stops bothering to type the program name in the quotes after **LOAD**, but this makes loading less reliable. If you have named the program, the ZX81 will ignore all others, even the tail of a previous program. In fact, if required, the ZX81 will search through a tape and load the named program. You must get the name *exactly* right — one letter or space wrong and nothing will be loaded.

SAVING DATA

Many computers use DATA and READ statements which allow program lines containing many items of data. The ZX81 does not have this facility, it is obviously tedious to put this data in by means of **LET** statements, or to input the data each time the program is run.

All is not lost, however! It's very important to realize that once you have run a program and put in data with **INPUT**, there are only three operations which will get rid of that data:

(1) Switching off the ZX81.
(2) Pressing **RUN** again.
(3) Pressing **CLEAR** (a little used key that erases all variables).

To make the program work without pressing **RUN** we have to use **GOTO** as a command. Type this short program:

```
 1Ø INPUT A
 2Ø INPUT B
 3Ø INPUT C
1ØØ PRINT A; B; C;" GO"
```

Now type the command **GOTO** 1ØØ — you'll get the 2/1ØØ report code meaning "variable not known". **RUN** the program and put in values of 1, 2, 3 for variables A, B, C — this time you'll get the expected output:

123 GO

Now if you command **GOTO** 1ØØ, you'll get exactly the same output — the data is still all there! Without doing anything else, **SAVE** the program in the usual way, and with it you have saved your data. If you want to check up on this, first unplug the ZX81 for a moment to remove the possibility of cheating! Then **LOAD** in the usual way, command **GOTO** 1ØØ, and the output:

123 GO

will confirm that the data is still there. If you type **RUN** at any stage, the data vanishes, and you will have to put it in again. One last point. When you are really pushed for memory space, you may find that this will save some useful bytes:

(1) Write the part of the program needed for putting in the data.
(2) Run the program and input the data.
(3) Delete the program written in (1) and write the part of the program that uses the data.
(4) Save program plus data, and use **GOTO** n to make the program work — never **RUN**!

WE LEARNED THESE IN CHAPTER 15

COMMANDS

LLIST or **LLIST** n to list a program on paper using the ZX Printer.
COPY to make a copy of the contents of the tv screen on paper, using the ZX Printer. This can also be used as a statement in a program.
SAVE to transfer programs from the ZX81 onto tape.
LOAD to put taped programs back into the ZX81.
GOTO n to execute a program from line n without clearing any data.

ANYTHING ELSE

How to save data on tape and use it again.

CHAPTER 16

Round and Round — Just Ten Times

THE FOR/NEXT LOOP

With a quick look back to Chapter 12, you could write a program to go around a loop exactly ten times, couldn't you?

```
1Ø LET J = Ø
2Ø LET J = J + 1
3Ø PRINT J;" TIMES ROUND THE LOOP"
4Ø IF J< = 1Ø. THEN GOTO 2Ø
5Ø PRINT
6Ø PRINT "STOPPED FOR A REST"
```

BASIC has special statements to do the same job — change the above program as follows:

```
Delete line 1Ø
2Ø FOR J = 1 TO 1Ø
4Ø NEXT J
```

Run it — the output is identical — **FOR/NEXT** is a wonderful time saver. To see how it works, study the complete program and the flow-chart opposite.

Here are some points about **FOR/NEXT** loops:

(1) N is the *loop control variable.* It may have any single letter name from A to Z, but steer clear of letters you are using elsewhere for ordinary variables.

(2) The numbers on either side of **TO** are the lower and upper limits for the loop control variable. As usual they may be numbers, variables, or expressions, but the ZX81 does not round off values in this case.

(3) The loop control variable is increased by 1 each time around the loop. Note that it finishes up 1 more than the upper limit for the loop.

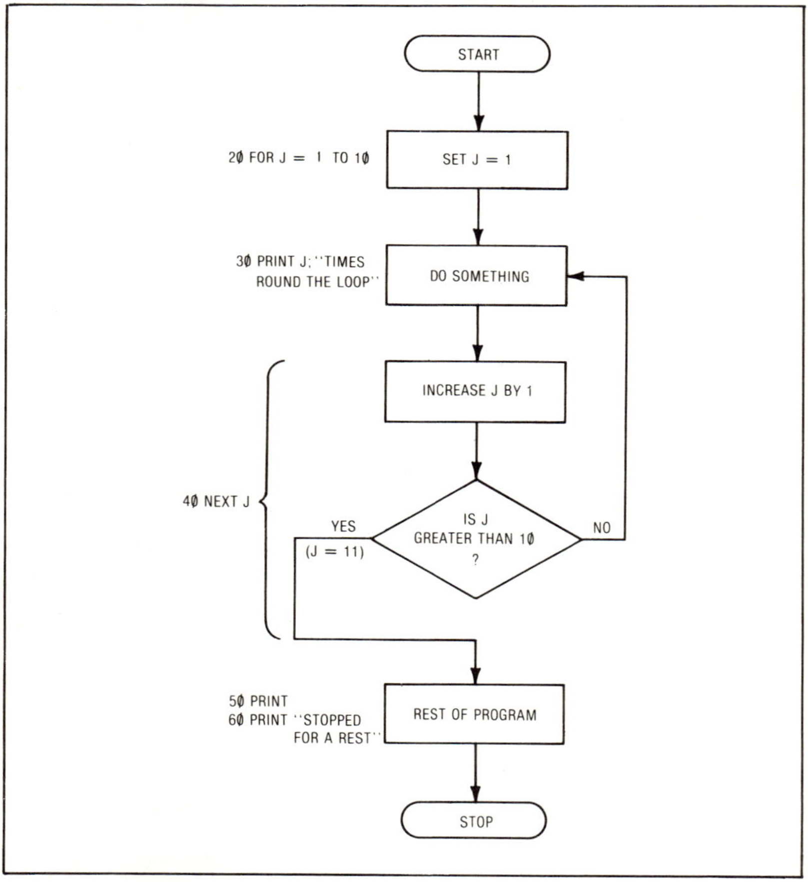

(4) Inside the loop may be any number of program lines with any of the usual statements. You can do anything you like which *uses* the value of N, so long as you don't change it. Remember that N increases by 1 each time around the loop.
(5) You may jump out of the loop with an **IF/THEN GOTO** statement, but don't jump into the middle of a **FOR/NEXT** LOOP — the ZX81 will not know what the loop control variable is.
(6) **FOR** without **NEXT** is incorrect but will be ignored. **NEXT** without **FOR** will stop the program with a 1/n or 2/n error.

Now try out your **FOR/NEXT** technique with this problem:

EXERCISE 16.1. SQUARE ROOT TABLE

Write a program to print out the whole numbers from Ø to 16 with their square roots alongside, under a suitable heading.

STEP TO STEP

Hold on tight for the next revelation — we don't *have* to increase by 1 each time around a **FOR/NEXT** loop! If we add the magic word **STEP**, we can increase by any regular amount we like, or decrease by using a negative step. Some examples:

FOR N = 1 **TO** 12 **STEP** 3
FOR J = 8 **TO** Ø **STEP** − 1
FOR K = P **TO** Q **STEP** 3*R
FOR L = Ø **TO** 5 **STEP** Ø.5

Try changing the appropriate line in your last square root program:

FOR N = Ø **TO** 16 **STEP** 2

and

FOR N = 16 **TO** Ø **STEP** − 2

Now try this exercise using **FOR/NEXT/STEP**:

EXERCISE 16.2. MULTIPLES

Write a program to print out all the multiples of 4 between Ø and 1ØØ, in four neat columns. Hint — use the current value of the loop control variable not only as the multiple of 4, but also to direct where it is printed on the line.

WE LEARNED THESE IN CHAPTER 16

STATEMENTS

FOR/TO/NEXT to go around a loop any given number of times.
STEP to specify increases or decreases in the loop control variable, other than + 1.

CHAPTER 17

Loops Within Loops

MULTIPLE LOOPS

In the last chapter, every program had one single **FOR/NEXT** loop. But the number of loops in a program is not limited — try this for a start:

```
10 FOR J = 0 TO 4
20 PRINT TAB J; "FIRST LOOP"
30 NEXT J
40 PRINT
100 FOR J = 10 TO 12
110 PRINT TAB J; "SECOND LOOP"
120 NEXT J
```

Notice that we used J for both loop control variables — quite in order for separate loops, and a useful memory saver.

Here is a different program — note the difference in output.

```
10 FOR J = 1 TO 3
20 PRINT "OUTSIDE LOOP"
30 FOR K = 1 TO 5
40 PRINT TAB 5; "INSIDE LOOP"
50 NEXT K
60 NEXT J
```

This time we have a "K loop" *inside* the "J loop" — we call these *nested loops.* You can use up to 26 nested loops, but they must obey two important rules:

(1) You must use different letters for the loop control variables.
(2) Inner loops must be completely inside outer loops — no overlapping at either end.

Remember those addition squares in school math? Here's a small example:

```
0    1    2
1    2    3
2    3    4
```

If you trace down from the 1 in the top row and along from the 2 in the left-hand column, your lines meet at 3, showing that 1 + 2 = 3. We can draw these squares neatly with the ZX81:

```
10 FOR J = 0 TO 5
20 FOR K = 0 TO 5
30 PRINT TAB 4*K; J + K
40 NEXT K
50 PRINT,,,,
60 NEXT J
```

Now an exercise for you to play with.

EXERCISE 17.1. MULTIPLICATION SQUARE

Here is a small multiplication square which works in the same kind of way:

```
1    2    3
2    4    6
3    6    9
```

Change the last program for the addition square, to draw out a multiplication square covering numbers from 1 up to 7.

SIMPLE GRAPHICS

Graphics and loops often go together, so let's have a look at the graphic blocks on the keyboard. Remember that you must press the **GRAPHICS** key first, and then again when you have finished. Each graphic block is a square the size of a letter, divided into four smaller squares which can be black, white, or (to a limited extent) gray. They are beautifully illustrated in your ZX81 manual. There are also inverse letters and some inverse symbols, and inverse space (black square) gets a lot of use. We can make the ZX81 print any of the graphic blocks as though they were letters — here's an 8 by 8 gray square as an example:

```
1ØØ PRINT "▒";
```

Type it and run it — one square drawn, 63 to go! Add these lines:

```
 9Ø FOR K = 1 TO 8
11Ø NEXT K
```

Brilliant! A row of 8 blocks this time. Add two more lines, to give us 8 of these rows:

```
 8Ø FOR J = 1 TO 8
13Ø NEXT J
```

We have 64 blocks now, but they're not exactly in the form of a square. What went wrong? That's right, it's the semicolon after each block that is printing them all in a continuous line. We need to jump to a new line after each set of 8 blocks — in other words at the end of each J loop. One more line will do it:

```
12Ø PRINT
```

and now your square is looking good, thanks to nested loops.

It's your turn now:

EXERCISE 17.2. RECTANGLE

Write a program to draw a black rectangle, 19 blocks wide and 5 blocks high.

Now modify your program so that it prints a title ''THIS IS A RECTANGLE'', in inverse graphics right in the middle of the rectangle.

There's plenty more to do with the graphics — to be continued in Chapter 23.

WE LEARNED THESE IN CHAPTER 17

Multiple loops and nested loops.
Simple graphics, using the graphics blocks.

CHAPTER 18

What a Friendly Machine!

Remember **LET** and **INPUT**? They were two ways of putting a *value* into a *numeric variable.* Wouldn't it be great to be able to do the same for words? Now for the good news, you can do all that and more! Here is a sample:

```
10 PRINT "TYPE YOUR NAME THEN PRESS ENTER"
20 INPUT A$
30 PRINT "THANK YOU"; A$
40 FOR J = 1 TO 200
50 NEXT J
60 PRINT,, "THATS A PRETTY NAME"
```

A$ is the big news — it's the name of a *string variable.* At line 20 the program stops, and the cursor [L] at the bottom of the screen tells us that the ZX81 is waiting for a string input. So we type in any characters we like (or even none at all, the empty string), press **ENTER**, and our string is pigeonholed under the label A$. We can now use A$ any time we wish, as in line 30. Lines 40 and 50 are an empty **FOR/NEXT** loop, a handy way of pausing in between outputs. You can use up to 26 string variables with names using any single letter from A to Z, followed by the $ sign.

If we add two more lines:

```
70 GOTO 10
25 CLS
```

we now have a *string input loop,* and we can continue typing names (pretty ones) as long as we like. These loops are somewhat hard to get out of, since whatever we type in is accepted by the ZX81 as a new string input. Try typing **STOP** for example. The solution is to remove the string input quotes at the bottom of the screen — pressing **EDIT** is the simplest way, or you can rub them out as usual. Now if you press **STOP** and then **ENTER** you will find that you are back in the command mode.

Now here is a program in which we use **LET** to define two string variables.

```
10 LET A$ = "INAUGURATION"
20 LET B$ = "STREET"
30 LET C$ = A$ + B$
40 LET N = 10
50 PRINT "WHO LIVES AT No."; N; C$; "?"
```

In line 30 we have joined together two string variables *(concatenated* is the official word), and put the result into a third string variable. In line 50 we have printed a whole mixture of items, literal strings, number and string variables, all on one line of the screen. We can print any of these items anywhere we like on the line by using ; , or **TAB** as usual.

WHAT CAN YOU DO WITH STRING VARIABLES?

As we've seen, you can print them, as often as you like, and you can join them together like a string of beads by using + (– will not work, by the way). You can also change them in a program, just like number variables. For example:

```
25 LET A$ = "WASHINGTON"
```

We've changed our mind about A$!

One more thing you can do is to *compare* string variables, either with each other or with literal strings, using our old friend **IF**. More lines for you to type:

```
 60 INPUT P$
 70 PRINT,, P$
 80 IF P$ = "THE PRESIDENT" THEN GOTO 100
 90 GOTO 50
100 PRINT,, "THATS RIGHT"
```

In line 80 we have used = to compare the input answer P$ with the literal string "THE PRESIDENT". Note that in BASIC, = means exactly equal — every letter, dot, comma, and space must be identical! Run the program and vary the input to check this. Try writing the program in a simpler way:

```
80 IF P$ <> "THE PRESIDENT" THEN GOTO 50
Delete line 90
```

Occasionally we use > and < to compare string variables. This program will show you exactly what happens:

```
 10 PRINT "TYPE A WORD"
 20 INPUT A$
 30 PRINT "NOW ANOTHER"
 40 INPUT B$
 50 PRINT,,A$; "COMES";
 60 IF A$ > B$ THEN GOTO 100
 70 PRINT "BEFORE";
 80 GOTO 110
100 PRINT "AFTER";
110 PRINT B$, "IN THE DICTIONARY"
```

Run the program and input ARK and ZOO, then ABRACADABRA and AARDVARK. Now you know what > means when applied to strings.

This chapter has taken our programming a long way forward. Here is a simple program to practice your string variables.

EXERCISE 18.1. FORM FILLING

Write a program requesting someone to type their name, age, and home town. Print out the information and thank the person nicely.

USING THE PRINTER AGAIN

Now that we know how to print numbers, literal strings, number and string variables on the screen (under the control of punctuation), and **TAB**, it is important to note that we can print all these on paper just as easily. We need the ZX Printer, which must have been plugged in before we switched the power on, and we use **LPRINT** in place of **PRINT** all through the program. You can even mix up **PRINT** and **LPRINT** statements. This program puts odd numbers on the tv screen and even numbers on paper:

```
 10 FOR J = 1 TO 20
 20 IF J/2 = INT (J/2) THEN GOTO 100
 30 PRINT J
 40 GOTO 200
100 LPRINT J
200 NEXT J
```

Now after running the program, change one line as follows:

```
100 LPRINT J;" ";
```

This time we are making the ZX81 print the even numbers all on one line. Notice how the printer saves them up till the end of the program, and then prints them all at once. The ZX Printer stores up its **LPRINT** items in a *buffer* store until there is some reason to print the current buffer contents and move on to the next line, for example:

end of program
current line full
last **LPRINT** item not followed by ; or ,
TAB number less than the current print position.

WE LEARNED THESE IN CHAPTER 18

STATEMENTS

LET to define a string variable.
INPUT to stop the program to input a string variable.
LPRINT to print any item on paper, using the ZX Printer.

ANYTHING ELSE

Printing and joining string variables.
Comparing string variables and strings using
IF with =, <>, > or <.

CHAPTER 19

Change Speed, Stop, and Pause

All the programs in this book so far will have worked for both ZX81 and ZX80 (with 8K ROM). However, while ZX81 owners have been watching the work in progress on their screens while the programs are running, ZX80 fans have had to sit in front of blank gray screens, waiting for a final printout.

With a ZX81 you can choose to run it like a ZX80 by typing the command **FAST**, and it then works at four times the speed of the usual **SLOW** mode. Indeed, you can get the best of both worlds by using **FAST** and **SLOW** as statements in your programs. In the following program, you can compare **FAST** and **SLOW** working:

```
 10 FAST
100 CLS
110 FOR J = 1 TO 40
120 LET C = EXP (LN J/3)
130 PRINT C,
140 NEXT J
200 STOP
210 SLOW
220 GOTO 100
```

The program first works out a set of 40 cube roots in **FAST** mode, and when they are all done it displays them (thanks to **STOP**). Now if you type **CONT**, it will change to **SLOW** mode and do the same work again.

The choice of **FAST** or **SLOW** is a matter of personal preference, but here is a rough guide:

FAST preferred:
- complicated calculations
- tedious printouts
- program writing, provided you don't mind the screen flashing each time you press a key.

SLOW preferred:
- most programs, especially those using graphics.

SLOW essential (in other words, ZX80 will not do)
- programs with moving graphics, bouncing balls, flashing words, and so on.

By the way, when you save a program you also save the mode the ZX81 happens to be in, whether **FAST** or **SLOW**. Make sure it's in the mode you want.

STOPPING YOUR PROGRAM

These things will make your program come to a stop:

(1) It has reached the end and stopped with a Ø/n report code.
(2) You have pressed **BREAK** and stopped it with a D/n code.
(3) A **STOP** statement was included in one of your program lines (9/n code).
(4) You have used up all the lines in the screen and stopped with a 5/n code.
(5) Some other error has stopped the program (various codes).
(6) It has reached an **INPUT** statement and is waiting for you to enter a number or a string.

The last is the most useful of all. You can use it to stop the program, look at the display on the screen, and restart when you are ready. Look at this program, which shows you how fast bacteria grow under favorable conditions. Doubling every 30 minutes is fairly typical, ignoring the fact that they also run out of food or die.

```
10 LET N = 1
20 LET T = 0
30 CLS
40 PRINT T; "HOURS HAVE GONE BY"
50 PRINT,, "YOUR CULTURE CONTAINS"; N; "BACTERIA"
60 LET T = T + 0.5
70 LET N = 2*N
80 PRINT,,,, "PRESS ENTER TO GO ON"
90 INPUT A$
100 GOTO 30
```

Notice how we could input anything at line 90, but the empty string (just pressing **ENTER**) is all that's needed to start the program moving again.

PROGRAM BRANCHING AND CRASHPROOFING

We can use a similar technique to allow a user the choice of branching to different parts of the program:

```
100 PRINT "TYPE YES OR NO"
110 INPUT A$
120 IF A$ = "YES" THEN GOTO 200
140 PRINT "YOU TYPED NO"
150 STOP
200 PRINT "YOU TYPED YES"
```

Run the program and obey the instructions, typing YES or NO obediently. Now be daring and type DONALD DUCK — the program stoutly declares "YOU TYPED NO"!

A warning — the world is full of clever turkeys who are out to try to make computers look silly. You must also think of the newcomers to computing — they'll be put off forever if they keep getting report codes and having to start again. All programmers are responsible for making their programs foolproof and vandalproof as far as possible. That is hard to do with 1K of memory, but at least remember the principle for later!

Let's patch up the last program by adding:

```
130 IF A$ <> "NO" THEN GOTO 110
```

Much better now — I've drawn two flowcharts to make it clear what is happening in each version. Over to you now:

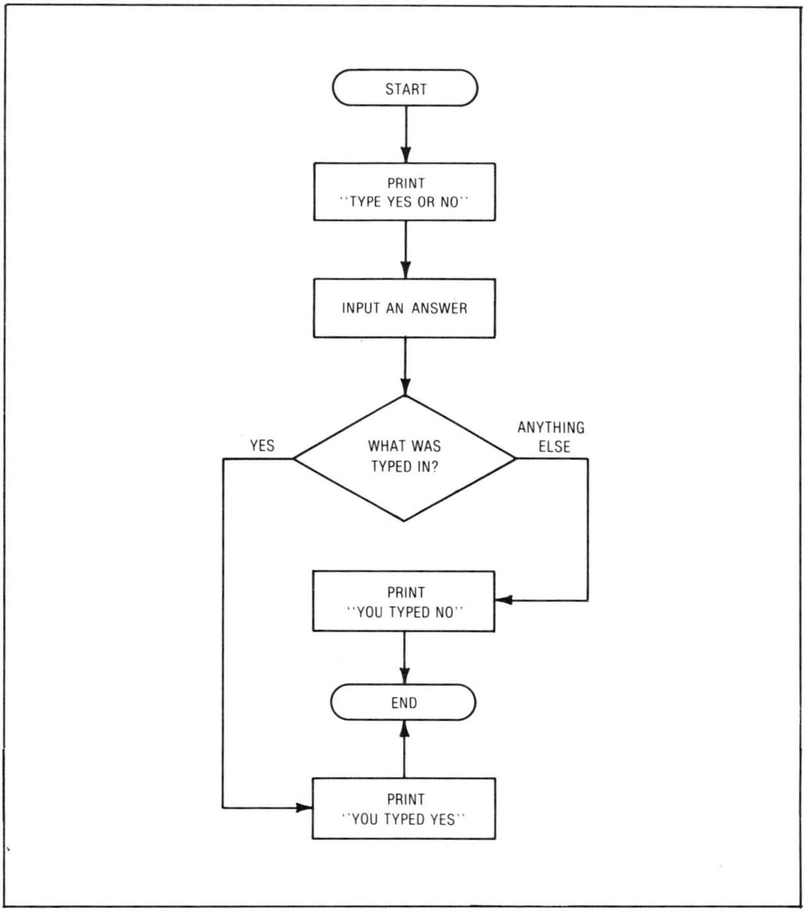

EXERCISE 19.1. CHOOSING NUMBERS

Write a foolproof program to ask the user to input a whole number between 1 and 100, and to print out the number together with its square.

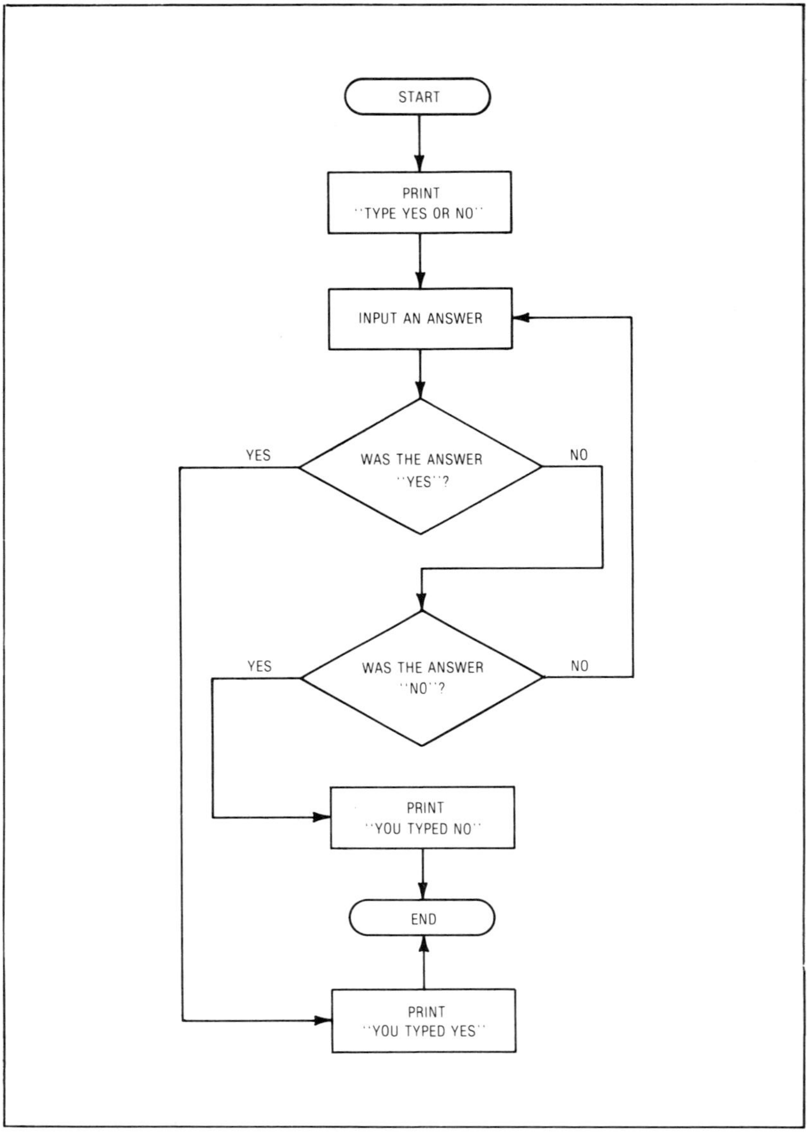

Include lines to make sure that it *is* a whole number and between 1 and 100. There is one input error you *cannot* guard against at present — what is it?

PAUSES IN PROGRAMS

ZX81 has a built-in pause statement — let's see how it works:

```
10 PRINT "HOW LONG?"
20 PRINT "TYPE NUMBER OF SECONDS"
30 INPUT S
40 PRINT S; "SECOND PAUSE STARTS NOW"
50 PAUSE S*60
60 PRINT "TIMES UP"
```

The statement **PAUSE** n gives a pause equal to n frames on the tv screen (at 60 per second in the US). It works in **SLOW** or **FAST** mode, but in **FAST**, or with a ZX80, the manual recommends that you follow each **PAUSE** statement with this line to avoid losing your program.

Line Number **POKE** 16437,255

I have not had this problem with **PAUSE** in **FAST** mode, but you have been warned! You can't pause for more than 32767 tv frames (nearly 11 minutes), and if n is bigger than this the pause is forever. However, if you press any key during a pause the program restarts at once, so this is another way of stopping a program to read the current display:

```
200 PRINT "PRESS ANY KEY TO GO ON"
210 PAUSE 40000
220 PRINT "BACK TO WORK"
230 GOTO 220
```

WE LEARNED THESE IN CHAPTER 19

COMMANDS

FAST to put the ZX81 into **FAST** mode.
SLOW to return the ZX81 to **SLOW** mode.

STATEMENTS

FAST and **SLOW** as above.
PAUSE n to give a pause in the program.

ANYTHING ELSE

When to use **FAST** and **SLOW** modes.
INPUT or **PAUSE** for temporary stops in the program.
Making the program branch, under control of a string input by the user.
Crashproof programs.

CHAPTER 20
A Chancy Business

RANDOM NUMBERS

There's a simple random number generator we've all used — the dice. This obeys certain obvious rules. It can only give numbers from 1 to 6. Unless it is loaded, or an odd shape, each of the numbers is equally likely to turn up. Finally, being a dumb piece of wood or plastic, it is not affected by anything that has happened before. We can turn these into general rules for random numbers:

(1) A random number is one drawn from a given set of numbers.
(2) Each number in the set is equally likely to be drawn.
(3) The draw is completely unaffected by previous draws.

ZX81 provides a random number function, **RND** — let's try it out:

```
100 FOR J = 1 TO 20
110 PRINT RND
120 NEXT J
```

Run it a few times — what do you notice? Sets of twenty numbers, each one bigger than 0 and less than 1, and they certainly look fairly random. In fact they are *pseudo-random numbers,* — each one is calculated in a clever way from the one before, so that rules (1) and (2) are obeyed. However, they always start with the same "seed" number when the ZX81 is switched on, and the same sequence of numbers will always be repeated (you can check this if you want to). Playing games with the same set of dice throws every time is a bit predictable, to say the least. Fortunately ZX81 provides a statement which sets a random "seed" number at the start:

```
10 RAND
```

Now you'll get a different set of random numbers each time you switch on the power and run (you can check this too!).

If we do want the ZX81 to throw dice, how are we going to convert our **RND** values into numbers from 1 to 6? Have a look at this:

Set of Numbers given by	*Smallest*	*Largest*
RND	0.000 . . .	0.999 . . .
RND*6	0.000 . . .	5.999 . . .
RND*6 + 1	1.000 . . .	6.999 . . .
INT (**RND***6 + 1)	1	6

So, change line 110 in our program:

```
110 PRINT INT (RND*6 + 1)
```

Now we really do seem to be throwing dice. By taking **RND**, multiplying it by one number and adding or subtracting another number, we can change it to any range of numbers we like.

EXERCISE 20.1. ROULETTE

Write a program to fill the screen with spins of a roulette wheel, which in the best games vary from 0 to 36. Check that 0 and 36 really do appear.

At the end of Chapter 11, we looked at various statements which needed numbers to go with them. You can often use random numbers, as with this constellation program:

```
10 FOR J = 0 TO 21
20 PRINT TAB RND*31; "*"
30 NEXT J
40 PAUSE 50
50 CLS
60 GOTO 10
```

Remember that we need not do anything to **RND***31 in line 20, it's automatically rounded to the nearest whole number between 0 and 31.

In the same way, we can use random numbers to define the size of a **FOR/NEXT** loop, though here no rounding off takes place and it may be advisable to convert the random numbers to integers. You try this one:

EXERCISE 20.2. RANDOM RECTANGLE

Write a program using nested **FOR/NEXT** loops to draw a rectangle of random size (length and breadth varying between 1 and 15).

RANDOM BRANCHING

We have learned how to stop a program and give the user a *choice* of two or more branches to go along. Using **RND**, we can remove the choice and let the branching happen by chance. Here's a simple example:

```
10 PRINT "YOU ARE WALKING HOME",,,
20 IF RND < .5 THEN GOTO 100
30 FOR J = 1 TO 15
40 PRINT TAB J; "           "
                    (GRAPHICS/SHIFT YYAHYY)
50 NEXT J
60 PRINT,, "YOU WENT THE PRETTY WAY"
70 GOTO 200
100 PRINT,, "SHORT CUT"
200 PRINT,, "YOU ARE HOME"
```

Another way of branching at random is to **GOTO** a random number. Here is a program which draws blocks out of a bag containing equal numbers of black, gray, and checked blocks.

```
 5Ø FOR J = Ø TO 5
 6Ø LET X = 1ØØ * INT (RND*3 + 1)
 7Ø GOTO X
1ØØ FOR K = 1 TO 3
11Ø PRINT TAB 5*J; " ███ " (3 of GRAPHICS/SPACE)
12Ø NEXT K
13Ø NEXT J
14Ø STOP
2ØØ FOR K = 1 TO 3
21Ø PRINT TAB 5*J; "▒▒▒ " (3 of GRAPHICS/SHIFT H)
22Ø NEXT K
23Ø NEXT J
24Ø STOP
3ØØ FOR K = 1 TO 3
31Ø PRINT TAB 5*J; " ▚▚▚ " (3 of GRAPHICS/SHIFT Y)
32Ø NEXT K
33Ø NEXT J
```

Notice that the last part of the program is repeated three times at lines 1ØØ, 2ØØ, and 3ØØ — bad programming and a waste of memory. We'll improve on this in the next chapter.

WE LEARNED THESE IN CHAPTER 20

STATEMENT

RAND to pick a random seed for calculation of random numbers.

FUNCTION

RND, a pseudo-random number between 0 and 1.

ANYTHING ELSE

Using random numbers.
Random branching in a program.

CHAPTER 21

Gone Out, Bizzy, Back Soon

SUBROUTINES

The statement **GOSUB** n is related to **GOTO** n and is extremely useful. It tells the ZX81,

(1) To go to the part of the program at line n.
(2) To do what it is told to there.
(3) To come back to the part of the program that it started from.

Here is a very simple demonstration:

```
100 PRINT "SUBROUTINE DEMO"
110 PRINT,, "JUST OFF TO SUBR 1000"
120 GOSUB 1000
130 PRINT "RETURNED"
140 PRINT,, "ON THE WAY TO SUBR 2000"
150 GOSUB 2000
160 PRINT "BACK AGAIN"
```

Run it now and see what happens. Well, it obeyed lines 100 to 120, went off to line 1000, found nothing there and stopped. We must write in the subroutines:

```
1000 PRINT TAB 5; "THIS IS SUBR 1000"
2000 PRINT TAB 5; "WE ARE AT SUBR 2000"
```

Not right yet — it went to line 1000 as planned, didn't go back again but went on to line 2000 and stopped. We need to put in the instructions to make it return from each subroutine — **RETURN**. We'll also put in a **STOP** to fence off the subroutines from the main program:

```
 900 STOP
1000 PRINT TAB 5; "THIS IS SUBR 1000"
1010 RETURN
2000 PRINT TAB 5; "WE ARE AT SUBR 2000"
2010 RETURN
```

Run the program and make sure it works. It's worth writing down the program lines in the order that they are used:

100, 110, 120, 1000, 1010, 130, 140, 150, 2000,
2010, 160, 900

Now that we've learned something about subroutines, we can write down some formal rules:

(1) At **GOSUB** n the ZX81 goes straight to line n (or to the next line if n does not exist). n may be a number, a variable or an expression.
(2) The ZX81 executes the subroutine just as though it is part of the main program.
(3) The subroutine must finish with a **RETURN** statement, which sends the ZX81 back to the line following the original **GOSUB** n statement.
(4) You may jump out of one subroutine into another, provided you are very clear-headed about what you are doing!
(5) It is often useful to have a conditional **GOSUB** in your program:
 IF something is true **THEN GOSUB** n.
(6) Put all your subroutines at the end of your program, and use **STOP** between main program and subroutines to avoid crashing into them.

We can often usefully include **GOSUB** in a loop — here is a new version of the random cube drawing program in the last chapter. It's much shortened by the use of **GOSUB**:

```
 10 FOR J = 0 TO 5
 20 LET X = 100 *INT (RND*3 + 1)
 30 FOR K = 1 TO 3
 40 GOSUB X
 50 NEXT K
 60 NEXT J
 90 STOP
100 PRINT TAB 5*J; " ███ " (3 of GRAPHICS/SPACE)
110 RETURN
200 PRINT TAB 5*J; " ▒▒▒ " (3 of GRAPHICS/SHIFT H)
210 RETURN
300 PRINT TAB 5*J; " ▚▚▚ " (3 of GRAPHICS/SHIFT Y)
310 RETURN
```

WHEN SHOULD WE USE SUBROUTINES?

As we already have seen, it makes sense to use a subroutine when we want to leave the main program at several points and do the same operation each time. Subroutines save both computer memory and programmers' time and effort.

Another reason for using subroutines is to make a long program easier to understand. We divide it up into:

A main program, which may be quite short.
A set of subroutines, labeled with **REM** statements.

It is also a great help to keep lists of your subroutine numbers and titles, and of all the variable names used.

Finally, you will write clever bits of program which you will want to use again. How much easier this will be if they are in the form of subroutines which can be transferred bodily to a new program.

EXERCISE 21.1. WATER TANK VOLUMES

Water tanks are cubes or cylinders for this exercise. Write a program that allows the user to choose one of these two shapes (rejecting all others), input the size and calculate the volume using one of these formulas:

$$\text{Volume of cube} = (\text{edge length})^3$$
$$\text{Volume of cylinder} = \text{Height} \times \pi \times \left(\frac{\text{diameter}}{2}\right)^2$$

WE LEARNED THESE IN CHAPTER 21

STATEMENTS

GOSUB n to direct the ZX81 to a subroutine at line n.
RETURN at the end of a subroutine to direct the ZX81 back to the main program.
STOP to fence off the subroutines from the main program.

CHAPTER 22

Speeding up the Input

So far, to input a number or a string, we have had to stop the program, type it in, and then press **ENTER** to go on. A new function, **INKEY$**, allows us to do this more quickly and smoothly, but it does have some limitations — for a start it needs the ZX81 in **SLOW** mode.

When the ZX81 meets **INKEY$**, it instantly checks every key on the board. If one key is being pressed, with or without **SHIFT**, the corresponding character is put into a single character string variable labeled **INKEY$**. Try this for a start:

```
100 PRINT INKEY$
```

A laborious way of printing?, wasn't it! You happened to be pressing **ENTER** at the time, which returns a ? character. Now we'll put **INKEY$** in a loop, to give you a chance to get your finger off **ENTER** and onto some other keys.

```
110 GOTO 100
```

Have fun pressing lots of keys, but remember that for each character printed on the screen, ZX81 has checked the whole keyboard and put a new character into **INKEY$**. By the way, you can't press **SPACE** or £ — ZX81 reads these as **BREAK**.

I think you've grasped the idea that **INKEY$** is an ephemeral thing — whenever you mention **INKEY$** in a program it produces a new one, so we have to develop various tricks to make use of it.

PROGRAM BRANCHING

Here is a smooth, fast version of the program with a choice of branches, like the one in Chapter 19.

```
 10 PRINT "GO ON OR STOP?"
 20 PRINT,, "PRESS G OR S"
 30 IF INKEY$ = "G" THEN GOTO 200
 40 IF INKEY$ = "S" THEN GOTO 100
 50 GOTO 30
100 PRINT,, "YOU STOPPED"
110 STOP
200 PRINT,, "YOU WENT ON"
```

Almost foolproof — press any key you like (except **BREAK**), and the ZX81 continues looping round lines 30/40/50 until G or S is pressed.

A PERMANENT RECORD OF INKEY$

In the program above, we used **INKEY$** and then forgot it, but sometimes we need to make a permanent record like this:

```
 10 PRINT "PRESS ANY KEY"
100 IF INKEY$ <>" "THEN GOTO 100
110 IF INKEY$ = " "THEN GOTO 110
120 LET A$ = INKEY$
130 PRINT "YOUR INKEY$ WAS" ; A$
```

That needs a little explaining! Line 100 holds up the program till *no* key is being pressed — giving you a chance to get your finger off **ENTER**. Then line 110 stops the program until a key *is* pressed, and finally line 120 puts the **INKEY$** character into A$. Run the program, and then type in the commands.

```
PRINT INKEY$ (it's gone)
PRINT A$ (it's still there)
```

With a few additions, we can use **INKEY$** to input strings of any specified length:

```
 10 PRINT "TYPE A THREE LETTER WORD"
 20 LET A$ = ""
100 FOR J = 1 TO 3
110 IF INKEY$ <> "" THEN GOTO 110
120 IF INKEY$ = "" THEN GOTO 120
130 LET A$ = A$ + INKEY$
140 NEXT J
150 PRINT "YOUR WORD WAS"; A$
```

Although you *can* juggle with **INKEY$** to input strings of unspecified length, this has little advantage over **INPUT**.

Here's a program that demonstrates another use for **INKEY$** and allows you to exercise its "interactive" side.

```
10 PRINT "MOVE ME"
20 LET A = 10
30 LET B = 15
40 PRINT AT A,B;"ME"
50 IF INKEY$ = "5" THEN LET B = B - 1
60 IF INKEY$ = "8" THEN LET B = B + 1
70 IF INKEY$ = "6" THEN LET A = A + 1
80 IF INKEY$ = "7" THEN LET A = A - 1
90 GOTO 40
```

This application of **INKEY$** is mostly used in games and simply demonstrates how a graphic configuration can be moved around the screen. The program is in need of some clean up which will be done in another program in a later chapter. To stop the movement of the graphic "ME" around the screen, press **BREAK**.

HOW ABOUT NUMBERS?

If you use your program above and type in 123, the result *looks* like a number but is really the string "123" so you cannot do any math operations on it. Luckily, ZX81 BASIC provides a function which turns suitable strings into numbers! Change and extend your program like this:

```
150 PRINT,, "STRING A$", "VAL A$"
160 PRINT A$, VAL A$
170 GOTO 10
```

Try putting in all sorts of strings, including some like these:

"123" "4.5" "6 + 7" "89A"

You have now discovered most of the rules for **VAL**:

(1) If a string consists entirely of characters which can be used in an arithmetical expression, **VAL** string will work out the expression and produce the answer. Suitable characters are:
- Numbers
- Names of variables previously defined
- Operators
- Full stop
- Functions
- Parentheses.

(2) Any other characters will stop the program with a C/n or 2/n error code.

(3) You can keep a permanent record of **VAL** string by putting it into a number variable:
LET A = **VAL** A$

ZX81 also provides another function which exactly reverses **VAL**, namely **STR$**.

STR$ number = "number"
STR$ 567 = "567"

This seemed a logical place to mention **STR$** — we'll use it later on.

Here's a well-known program for you to write, using **INKEY$** and **VAL**:

EXERCISE 22.1. NUMBER GUESSING

Write a program to generate a random number between 10 and 99. Ask the user to type in a guess, and then tell him whether the guess is too low, too high, or correct. With 1K of memory, you'll need to limit the guesses to about eight.

WE LEARNED THESE IN CHAPTER 22

FUNCTIONS

INKEY$ to allow a single character string to be input without stopping the program.
VAL to change a suitable string into a number.
STR$ to change a number into a string.

CHAPTER 23

Son of Graphics

In Chapter 17 we drew simple pictures by using **PRINT** with graphics blocks in quotes. Each graphic block was made of four small squares (pixels) which could be black, white, or gray.

PLOTTING POINTS

We can use the statement **PLOT** (X,Y) to black in a single pixel anywhere on the screen. Try this demonstration program:

```
 20 PRINT "PLOT X,Y DEMO"
 30 PRINT,, "Ø TO 63 POINTS ALONG — THATS X"
 40 PRINT,, "AND Ø TO 43 POINTS UP — THATS Y"
 50 PRINT,, "WHAT IS X (Ø TO 63)? X = ";
 60 INPUT X
 70 PRINT X,,, "NOW Y (Ø TO 43)?"
 80 INPUT Y
 90 CLS
100 PLOT X,Y
110 PRINT X; ",";Y
120 INPUT A$
130 CLS
140 GOTO 50
```

If you run the program it should explain itself. Notice how the **PRINT** position in line 11Ø is immediately after the **PLOT** position in line 1ØØ.

The **CLS** in line 13Ø is a bit of a sledgehammer to remove one point! We can take it out more delicately by using **UNPLOT**, the reverse of **PLOT**.

```
130 UNPLOT X,Y
```

Notice how again the **PRINT** position follows right after the **UNPLOT** position.

PLOTTING LINES

A single black blob is not a lot of use, but watch what happens when we put it into a loop:

```
10 FOR J = 0 TO 63
20 PLOT J, 0
90 NEXT J
```

The start of a picture frame! Now we need a bar along the top of the screen. Can you work it out? That's right:

```
30 PLOT J,43
```

The rest of the frame is up to you:

EXERCISE 23.1. VERTICAL LINES

Add four more lines to the present program to draw the two verticals of the picture frame. There's a problem with your 1K of memory, by the way.

Oblique lines are not quite so successful, but let's see what we can do:

```
 10 FOR J = 0 TO 43
 20 PLOT J,0
 30 PLOT J,43
 40 PLOT 0,J
 50 PLOT 43,J
 60 PLOT J,J
 70 PLOT J,43—J
100 NEXT J
```

Put in lines 20 to 70 one by one, and run after each addition to check which program line draws which line on the screen.

If you want, you can use **PLOT** in nested loops to black out whole slabs of the screen, though it's a little slow.

```
10 FOR J = 0 TO 63
20 FOR K = 0 TO 41
30 PLOT J,K
40 NEXT K
50 NEXT J
```

We can wipe the whole screen as usual with:

```
60 CLS
```

However, if we halve the rectangle to release more memory, we can wipe it out in a more leisurely way — the Danish blue cheese method:

```
10 LET K = 0
20 FOR J = 0 TO 43
30 FOR K = 0 TO K
40 PLOT J,K
50 NEXT K
60 NEXT J
70 LET X = RND*43
80 UNPLOT X, RND*(X + 1)
90 GOTO 70
```

MIXING PRINT WITH GRAPHICS

As we know, the **PRINT** position follows immediately after the last **PLOT** or **UNPLOT** point, which can be inconvenient. Luckily ZX81 will let us print anywhere we like on the screen by using:

PRINT AT line number, column number; string or number

Line numbers go from Ø at the top of the screen to 21 at the bottom. Column numbers are the same as **TAB** numbers, Ø to 31. Here is a demonstration game to get you used to the **PRINT AT** positions:

```
 1Ø PRINT TAB 7; "PRINT AT DEMO"
 2Ø PAUSE 2ØØ
1ØØ CLS
11Ø PRINT "PUT A FINGER ON THESE POINTS"
12Ø PAUSE 2ØØ
13Ø LET L = INT (RND*22)
14Ø LET C = INT (RND*32)
15Ø CLS
16Ø PRINT "PRINT AT"; L; ","; C
17Ø PAUSE 4ØØ
18Ø PRINT AT L, C; "*"
19Ø GOTO 12Ø
```

Remember that any further printing follows right after the **PRINT AT** item, according to the usual punctuation rules. If you want to go back to the top of the screen, you'll have to use another **PRINT AT**.

PRINT AT is also useful for erasing bits of the screen — all you need to do is to print spaces at the positions you want to erase:

```
1ØØ FOR J = Ø TO 21
11Ø PRINT AT J, J; J
12Ø NEXT J
2ØØ PRINT AT Ø, 4; "ERASING THE ODD NUMBERS"
21Ø FOR J = 1 TO 21 STEP 2
22Ø PRINT AT J, J; " "
23Ø NEXT J
```

Here are some simple exercises using **PLOT** and **PRINT AT**:

EXERCISE 23.2. CALLING CARD

Write a program to print a black calling card in the center of the screen, with your name and address in inverse letters.

EXERCISE 23.3. ''ON WE GO'' SUBROUTINE

A very useful subroutine to stop the program until **ENTER** is pressed. Print the prompt ''PRESS **ENTER**'' at the bottom right of the screen, put in an **INPUT** pause, then wipe the bottom line only and **RETURN**.

GRAPHICS WITH THE ZX PRINTER

The simple graphics of Chapter 17, in which graphic block arrangements are printed line by line, can be recorded on paper by simply changing **PRINT** statements to **LPRINT**. On the other hand, **LPRINT AT** will not work, it behaves more or less like **LPRINT TAB**. If you think about it, **PRINT AT** may be asking the ZX81 to go back along a line, or to move up to some line previously printed — the ZX Printer cannot cope with this! Nor will **PLOT** produce any result with the ZX Printer — what can we do to make a permanent record of our beautiful graphics?

We met the answer in Chapter 15, simply use the keyword **COPY**, either as a command or a statement, and the ZX Printer will make a faithful copy on paper of the current screen contents — **PLOT** points, **PRINT AT** items and all.

WE LEARNED THESE IN CHAPTER 23

STATEMENTS

PLOT X, Y to black in a pixel at the coordinates X, Y.
UNPLOT X, Y to erase the pixel at the coordinates X, Y.
PRINT AT line number, column number; to print an item at any position on the screen, regardless of anything printed before.
COPY to make a permanent record on paper of the current screen contents, including all graphics and **PRINT AT** items.

ANYTHING ELSE

Loops containing **PLOT** to draw lines and blocks on the screen.
PRINT AT line, column; ''   '' to erase sections of the screen.

CHAPTER 24
Playing With Strings

There is a theory that, given infinite time and paper, a set of chimpanzees would eventually type the complete works of Shakespeare. Let's try:

```
10 RAND
90 CLS
100 FOR J = 1 TO 80
200 FOR K = 1 TO INT (RND*8 + 1)
210 LET A = INT (RND*26 + 38)
220 PRINT CHR$ A;
300 NEXT K
310 IF RND < .07 THEN PRINT ".";
350 PRINT " ";
400 NEXT J
500 PRINT
510 PRINT,, "PRESS ENTER"
520 INPUT A$
530 GOTO 90
```

I suppose the theory is all right, but you'll need a lot of patience! The important lines to look at are 210, which generates a random number between 38 and 63, and line 220, which prints a new function.

CHR$ A is the character which has the code number A, and if you look at the Appendix of your operating manual, you will find that 38 to 63 are the code numbers for A to Z.

We can use **CHR$** to see every character in the ZX81 repertoire, all 255 of them:

```
 10 LET K = 0
 20 FOR J = 1 TO 8
 30 FOR K = K TO K + 7
 40 PRINT CHR$ K;" ";
 50 NEXT K
 60 PRINT,,
 70 NEXT J
 80 PRINT,, "PRESS ENTER"
 90 INPUT A$
100 CLS
110 GOTO 20
```

You will see a whole mixture of graphic blocks, numbers, symbols, letters, keywords, functions, and inverse characters. The second page consists mostly of ?s — these are either unused characters or commands like **ENTER** which print nothing on the screen.

Two more useful string functions are **CODE** and **LEN**, and this program makes it pretty clear what they do:

```
10 PRINT "INPUT SOME WORDS"
20 PRINT "W$";TAB 10;"CODE W$";TAB 20;"LEN W$"
30 INPUT W$
40 PRINT,, W$;TAB 10;CODE W$;TAB 20;LEN W$
50 GOTO 30
```

Run the program and input words like APPLE, ANT, A, BEETLE, BUN, B. Try words consisting of spaces, and also the empty string. By now you will have discovered that **CODE** of a string gives "the code number of the first character in that string." **LEN** of a string is equal to "the number of characters (including spaces) in the string" — in other words, length of the string.

CHOPPING UP STRINGS

ZX81 has a simple but very useful way of *slicing* strings. As soon as a string or a string variable is typed in, its characters are each numbered, starting at 1, continuing 2, 3, . . ., and ending with the last character which has the same number as **LEN**. For example:

LET Z$ = "CAKE"　　　**LEN** Z$ = 4
Z$(1) = "C" Z$(2) = "A" Z$(3) = "K" Z$(4) = "E"

We can slice out any characters we like from a string by using the function:

string (m **TO** N)

Try it out with this program:

```
 10 PRINT "SLICING SPORTSMAN"
 20 LET A$ = "SPORTSMAN"
100 PRINT "INPUT TWO NUMBERS, 1 TO 9"
110 PAUSE 300
120 CLS
130 INPUT M
140 INPUT N
150 PRINT,, "SPORTSMAN(";M;" TO ";N;") = ";A$ (M TO N)
160 GOTO 130
```

If you input various pairs of numbers, you'll find that the first number must not be less than 1, and the second number must not be greater than 9 (**LEN** "SPORTSMAN" = 9).

You can, if you wish, chop out part of one string, and put into another string variable for future use. Type these commands, after running the program above:

LET B$ = A$ (2 **TO** 8)
PRINT A$, B$

You may only require a single character from your original string, and in this case you can drop the **TO**. Try typing a few commands like:

PRINT A$(1) **PRINT** A$(2) **PRINT** A$(9)

Again, the lower limit is 1 and the upper limit is **LEN** A$. Let's use this method to print your choice of word in all sorts of ways:

```
 10 PRINT "INPUT ANY WORD"
 20 INPUT W$
 30 CLS
100 FOR J = 1 TO LEN W$
110 PRINT W$(J); "";
120 NEXT J
```

That was straightforward, but now change line 100 to:

```
100 FOR J = LEN W$ TO 1 STEP - 1
```

And now let's print your word in inverse letters. We make use of the fact that the **CODE** of an inverse letter is 128 higher than the **CODE** of the original letter:

```
110 PRINT TAB 1;CHR$ (CODE W$(J) + 128)
```

Sorry, we've got it upside down now! Add these lines to march the letters into their correct places:

```
200 FOR J = 1 TO LEN W$
210 FOR K = 0 TO J - 1
220 PRINT AT LEN W$ - J + K,K + 1; CHR$ (CODE W$(J)
          + 128)
230 PRINT AT LEN W$ - J + K - 1,K; " "
240 NEXT K
250 NEXT J
```

Here's an exercise in which you can try out slicing for yourself:

EXERCISE 24.1. ANTS

Ants are words which begin with ''ANT'' or end with ''ANT''. Write a program which asks for words to be input, checks them, lists them on the screen if they are ants, or rejects them if they are not.

WE LEARNED THESE IN CHAPTER 24

FUNCTIONS

CHR$ n , equal to the character which has the code number n.
CODE s , equal to the code number of the first character in string s.
LEN s , equal to the number of characters in string s.
s (m **TO** n) , equal to a slice from string s, from the m th character to the n th character.
s (n) , equal to the n th character from string s.

CHAPTER 25

In Glorious Array

DUMMY VARIABLES

We have learned how to do all sorts of things to numbers and strings. Sometimes we need to keep a record of the original number or string, using a dummy variable, so that we can refer to it later. Here's a simple example.

```
 10 LET B$ = ""
100 PRINT "TYPE A WORD"
110 INPUT A$
120 CLS
130 PRINT "YOU TYPED";A$
140 IF A$ = B$ THEN GOTO 300
200 PRINT "THATS A CHANGE"
210 PRINT "IT WAS";B$;"LAST TIME"
220 GOTO 400
300 PRINT "BORING — SAME AS LAST TIME"
400 LET B$ = A$
410 GOTO 100
```

We have an **INPUT** loop around lines 100 to 410, and variable A$ is changed each time we go around the loop. However, in line 400 we put A$ into a dummy variable B$, so that we can compare this with the new A$ next time around. We can do exactly the same with number variables, of course.

ARRAYS OF NUMBERS

We know how to keep a permanent record of one number by giving it a variable name. Now suppose we want to keep a record of a *set of numbers* that have something in common — for example, in a dice throwing experiment, the number of ones, twos, threes, fours, fives, and sixes we have thrown. We can do this by setting up a *single dimension array,* using the statement **DIM**:

```
10 DIM D(6)
```

If we run this program, we have now created six variables:

D(1)   D(2)   D(3)   D(4)   D(5)   D(6)

and each one of them has been set to zero. Check this by typing commands like: **PRINT** D(3)

An array must have a name consisting of a single letter. It can have as many members as you like, subject to available memory, and each member has a different subscript number in parentheses, starting with 1, to distinguish it from all the others. Note that D(0) does not exist.

On with the program — we'll randomize, and then throw the dice sixty times:

```
 20 RAND
100 FOR J = 1 TO 60
110 LET T = INT (RND*6 + 1)
200 NEXT J
```

Now for the cunning bit — this is where the subscripts come in. If we throw a five, we need to add one on to D(5), the total of fives thrown.

```
120 LET D(T) = D(T) + 1
```

If T happens to be a five, then this is the same as saying:

```
LET D(5) = D(5) + 1
```

The next T might be three, and we would add one on to D(3), and so on. Now we need to print out our results:

```
 90 PRINT "WAIT"
300 PRINT "60 DICE THROWS",,,,
310 FOR J = 1 TO 6
320 PRINT TAB 5;D(J);" ";J;" S",,
330 NEXT J
```

Finally we can stop to display the results, and then back to **DIM** in line 10 to reset all the array variables to zero and start again:

```
400 PRINT "PRESS N/L FOR MORE"
410 INPUT A$
420 GOTO 10
```

Later on, with moving graphics, we'll rewrite this program to give a compulsive race game.

MULTIDIMENSION ARRAYS

Imagine that we are renting fifteen camper vans to vacationers in the month of August. We arrange the vans in three rows, and each row has five vans in it.

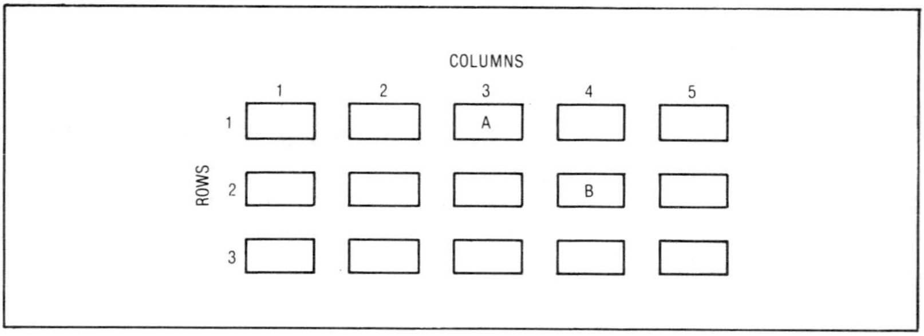

We can name a van uniquely by giving its ROW and then its COLUMN. For example, van A is (1,2) — ROW 1 and COLUMN 2. Van B is (2,4) and so on.

ZX81 will do exactly the same operation using **DIM**:

```
10 DIM V(3,5)
```

Run the program, this time we have set up 15 variables, arranged like the vans in a 3 × 5 array (see the previous Figure), each one set to zero:

V(1,1) = 0   V(1,2) = 0   and so on.

Now we can write a camper rental program, if we say that:

V(m,n) = 0 means a vacant van and V(m,n) = 1 means a booked van.

```
 20 PRINT "WHICH VAN DO YOU WANT?"
 30 PRINT,, "WHICH ROW (1 TO 3)?";
 40 INPUT R
 50 PRINT R
 60 PRINT "WHICH COLUMN (1 TO 5)?";
 70 INPUT C
 80 PRINT C
 90 PAUSE 200
100 IF V(R,C) = 1 THEN GOTO 200
110 PRINT,, "VAN (";R;"";C;") IS FREE"
120 LET V(R,C) = 1
130 PRINT,, "I HAVE RENTED IT FOR YOU"
140 PRINT,, "NEXT CUSTOMER PLEASE PRESS N/L"
150 GOTO 220
200 PRINT,, "SORRY, VAN (";R;",";C;") IS TAKEN"
210 PRINT,, "PRESS N/L TO TRY ANOTHER"
220 INPUT A$
230 CLS
240 GOTO 20
```

We are not limited to two dimensions, except by our available memory.

Each of the campers could be left out for each of the twelve months, needing a 3 × 5 × 12 array. This program would start

```
10 DIM V(3,5,12)
```

but you will have to write the rest!

Here is an array problem for you to try:

EXERCISE 25.1. SIMPLE COWS AND BULLS

This is the well-known game in which you have to guess a four-digit number. After your guess you are told how many of the digits you guessed exactly right (bulls). The general scheme is this:

Generate four random digits between 1 and 6 and put them in a single dimension array.
Ask the player to guess the number.
Input his guess as a string variable.
Compare the digits of his guess, one by one, with the digits in your array (remember **VAL**!).
Tell him how many bulls he scored.

WE HAVE LEARNED THESE IN CHAPTER 25

STATEMENTS

DIM to reserve space for an array of numbers and to set them all to zero.
e.g., **DIM** A(n) for a single-dimension array with n members.
DIM A(m,n) for a two-dimension array with m × n members.

ANYTHING ELSE

Dummy variables to provide a memory for variables which would otherwise be lost.

CHAPTER 26

Arrays of Strings

We found out about arrays of numbers in the last chapter. Arrays of strings are set up in much the same way. We already know that a string variable is equivalent to a single-dimension string of characters. For instance:

```
20 LET A$ = "CAT"
```

Run the program and type these commands:

```
PRINT A$(1) (this gives C)
PRINT A$(2) (this gives A)
PRINT A$(3) (this gives T)
```

If we put in a **DIM** statement:

```
10 DIM A$(5)
```

we have merely reserved space for one five-character string called A$, set all the characters to empty spaces, and then inserted the string "CAT". We can check this by adding:

```
30 FOR J = 1 TO 3
40 FOR K = 1 TO 5
50 PRINT A$(K)
60 NEXT K
70 NEXT J
```

There are five spaces available, but we have only filled three of them. Now we'll change the **DIM** statement — better type **NEW** and start again.

```
10 DIM B$(7,5)
```

This time we have reserved space for an array of seven strings, each one of five characters as before. Let's start putting in some actual strings:

```
20 LET B$(1) = "CAT"
30 LET B$(2) = "DOG"
40 LET B$(4) = "MOUSE"
```

and then printing them out:

```
100 FOR J = 1 TO 7
110 PRINT B$(J);
120 NEXT J
```

Notice that in defining members of this string array (lines 20 to 40), and in using them (line 110), we only type one subscript number, to say which of the strings we are talking about. The second subscript number is only used once — in the **DIM** statement — to fix the maximum length of each member of the array. What happens if we try to put in a longer string than we have allowed for?

```
50 LET B$(5) = "ELEPHANT"
```

ZX81 makes no objection, it merely refuses to print any characters after the first five! If you really need more than "ELEPH", you'll need to change the **DIM** statement. Maybe this is why the code on my driving license refers to a fellow called "NORMA"!

MULTIDIMENSION STRING ARRAYS

Just as easy, but a bit heavy on memory. Type the commands **NEW** and then **DIM** C$(4,3,8). This makes room for an array of 4 × 3 strings. Once again, the last subscript number is to fix the maximum length of the strings, and only appears in the **DIM** statement. When defining or using members of the array, we only use the first two numbers.

LET C$(2,3) = "ELEPHANT"
PRINT C$(2,3)

NAMING STRING ARRAYS

A string array may have any single-letter name, followed by $ and then the subscript numbers. A name like A$, for instance, can only be used for *one* string array. If you write a second **DIM** A$(m,n,..) you simply cancel the original **DIM** and replace it with this new one. But you can, if you want to, use all of these variables in a single program:

A (number variable)	A$ (string variable)
A (n,. . .) (number array)	A$ (n,. . .) (string array)

CHOPPING MEMBERS OF A STRING ARRAY

Assuming that you still have your C$(2,3) = "ELEPHANT" in memory, try typing these commands:

PRINT C$(2,3,1)
PRINT C$(2,3,2)
PRINT C$(2,3,8)

So obviously if you type in one extra subscript number, you simply pull that particular character out of the string variable. If you want larger slices, do it like this:

```
PRINT C$(2,3)(2 TO 7)
```

Now for some exercises using string arrays:

EXERCISE 26.1. TEST RESULTS

You have a class of six children — put their names into a string array. Write a program which asks for:

The name of the test.
The maximum possible mark.
Each child's mark (use a number array).

The output should consist of a title and a list of names and percentages.

EXERCISE 26.2. ONE-ARMED BANDIT

Set up a string array containing six fruit machine items (cherry, lemon, etc.). Generate three random numbers and use these to print three of the fruits across the screen. Check for a jackpot — three fruits that are the same.

WE LEARNED THESE IN CHAPTER 26

STATEMENTS

DIM A$(m,n. . .) to set single or multidimension string arrays. The last (extra) subscript number fixes the maximum length of each member of the array.

ANYTHING ELSE

Slicing out parts of string array members.

CHAPTER 27
Very Logical

We started this in Chapter 12 with **IF . . . THEN** — now let's take it a little further. Here is a picture of a water tank with some pretty weird plumbing. It has four water valves labeled A$, B$, Y$, and Z$.

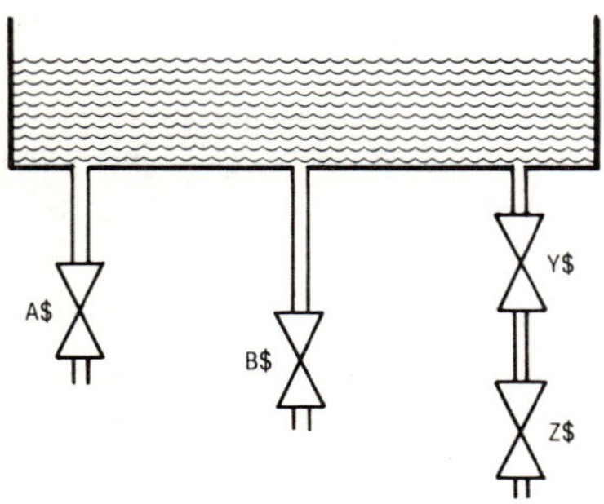

It's a simple chemical engineering problem. We have to write a program to warn us when water is running away through an open valve. We'll deal with A$ first:

```
10 PRINT "SET YOUR VALVES NOW",, "O = OPEN S = SHUT"
20 PRINT,, "A$ is? ";
30 INPUT A$
```

```
 40 PRINT A$
150 IF A$ = "O" THEN GOTO 1000
200 PRINT  "All OK"
210 PRINT AT 21,0; "PRESS N/L FOR MORE OR S TO STOP"
220 INPUT X$
230 IF X$ = "S" THEN STOP
240 CLS
250 GOTO 10
1000 PRINT
1010 FOR J = 1 TO 5
1020 PRINT "DING DONG"
1030 NEXT J
1040 PRINT,, "WATER RUNNING OUT"
1050 GOTO 210
```

Run the program, open and close A$, and make sure the alarm is working properly. Now for the B$ valve.

```
50 PRINT "BS IS? ";
60 INPUT B$
70 PRINT B$
```

Now we need a line like 150 to test whether B$ is open, but wait a minute . . . we can *include* B$ in line 150:

```
150 IF A$ = "O" OR B$ = "O" THEN GOTO 1000
```

Did it work? Sure did! The alarm goes off if either A$ or B$ is left open. Two more valves to go now:

```
 80 PRINT "Y$ IS? ";
 90 INPUT Y$
100 PRINT Y$
110 PRINT "Z$ IS? ";
120 INPUT Z$
130 PRINT Z$
```

We'll need to think hard about this — if either one of valves Y$ and Z$ is closed then we're still holding water. We only need the alarm if they are both open, so:

```
160 IF Y$ = "O" AND Z$ = "O" THEN GOTO 1000
```

Run the program again, and open and shut all the valves to test it out thoroughly. Then replace lines 150 and 160 with one single gloriously logical line:

```
150 IF A$ = "O" OR B$ = "O" OR Y$ = "O" AND Z$ = "O"
    THEN GOTO 1000
```

which works just as well. There is a flowchart for this program shown opposite.

PRIORITIES

These long logical statements need clear thinking. They depend on the fact that the ZX81 tests the statements in a specific order, giving **AND** priority over **OR**. As with arithmetical expressions, we can change the priority, or give it emphasis, by adding parentheses. For example this line:

```
150 IF A$ = "O" OR B$ = "O" OR (Y$ = "O" AND Z$ = "O")
    THEN GOTO 1000
```

has exactly the same effect as before, but it is easier to understand.

This is the time to mention that ZX81 has logical **NOT** available, though it seems to be superfluous because:

IF NOT A = B is the same as IF A <> B
IF NOT X > = Y is the same as IF X < Y
and so on.

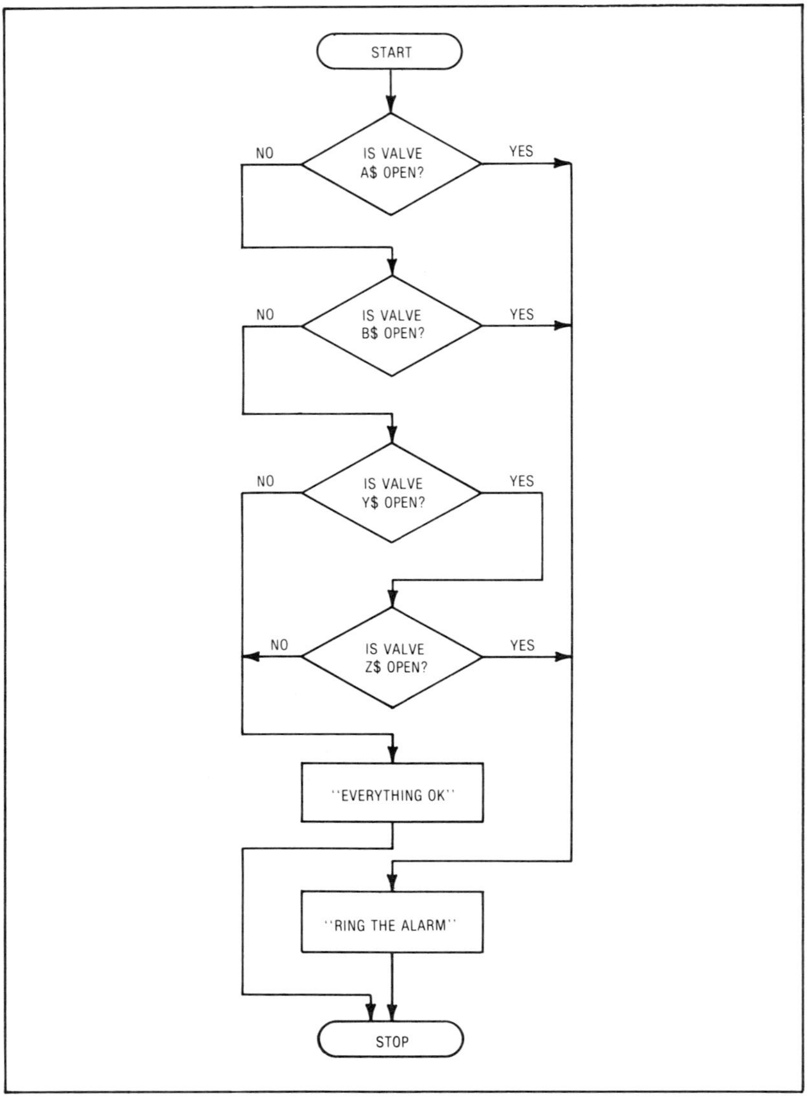

Also there are logical values which go with **AND, OR, NOT** — these are dealt with in Chapter 10 of the ZX81 operating manual. They should be considered as time- and memory-savers for advanced programmers, they do not do anything which cannot be done with statements already covered in this book.

Now try out your own logic.

EXERCISE 27.1. WATER TANK MARK 2

We've scrapped the old plumbing system — always thought it was rubbish! The tank is now fitted with a single branched outlet pipe fitted with three valves A$, B$, and C$. Change the input lines to fit these valves, and then type in this new logic line:

```
150 IF A$ = "O" AND (B$ = "O" OR C$ = "O") THEN GOTO
    1000
```

Run the program, open and shut the various valves, and deduce the new layout of pipes and valves.

WE LEARNED THESE IN CHAPTER 27

Logical statements **AND, OR** to use with the **IF** . . . **THEN** statement.

AND has priority over **OR**.

Parentheses to change or emphasize priority.

Chapter 28

Graphics Ride Again!

This chapter is concerned with moving graphics, which must be run in **SLOW** mode on the ZX81. Users of ZX80s will have to skip on to the next chapter.

FLASHING LIGHTS

If we want to emphasize special words on the screen, we can use inverse graphics, or flash the words, or both as in this subroutine:

```
 100 GOSUB 1000
 900 STOP
1000 REM**CORRECT ANSWER
1010 FOR J = 1 TO 20
1050 PRINT AT 15,20;"RIGHT"     (inverse characters)
1100 PRINT AT 15,20;"     "     (five spaces)
1200 NEXT J
```

As it stands, this program gives a fast flickering effect, it needs slowing down. Either insert **PAUSE** statements, or for a really smooth display use empty loops:

```
1060 FOR K = 1 TO 10
1070 NEXT K
1110 FOR K = 1 TO 10
1120 NEXT K
```

BOUNCING BALLS

For a start we'll draw bits of floor and ceiling for the ball to bounce between:

```
100 FOR J = 20 TO 40
110 PLOT J,1
120 PLOT J,42
130 NEXT J
```

Next we'll print the ball, fairly near the ceiling:

```
 10 LET V = 1
200 PRINT AT V,15;"O"
```

Now to move the ball down the screen:

```
 20 LET VV = 1
150 LET V = V + VV
400 GOTO 150
```

A nasty looking trail of Os — we'll have to rub them out as we go.

```
300 PRINT AT V,15;" "
```

A bit better that time, but the ball seems to be made of lead! To make it bounce we must change the sign of VV at the floor, and then again at the ceiling:

```
250 IF V = 20 OR V = 1 THEN LET VV = - VV
```

Success! It will bounce until you switch off or press **BREAK**.

Now we'll extend the program into two dimensions, to give the rudiments of a tv game. The idea is the same, but this time we are changing both the line number and the column number each time around the loop. We shall have to bounce inside a small rectangle to avoid running out of memory, and we start the ball at a random position:

```
 10 LET VV = 1
 20 LET HH = 1
 30 LET V = INT (RND*13 + 1)
 40 LET H = INT (RND*19 + 1)
210 FOR J = 1 TO 42
220 PLOT J,42
230 PLOT J,13
240 NEXT J
250 FOR J = 14 TO 41
260 PLOT 1,J
270 PLOT 42,J
280 NEXT J
300 LET H = H + HH
310 LET V = V + VV
320 PRINT AT V,H;"O"
330 IF H = 20 OR H = 1 THEN LET HH = -HH
340 IF V = 14 OR V = 1 THEN LET VV = -VV
350 PRINT AT V,H;" "
360 GOTO 300
```

CIRCLING SATELLITES

This program prints a star in the middle of the screen, and then uses **PLOT** to put a planet into orbit:

```
 10 PRINT "RADIUS? 3 UP TO 20"
 20 INPUT R
 30 PRINT AT 11, 15;"*"
 40 LET A = 0
100 UNPLOT 30 + R * SIN A,20 + R*COS A
110 LET A = A + .2
120 PLOT 30 + R * SIN A,20 + R*COS A
130 GOTO 100
```

This diagram shows you how the trigonometry works:

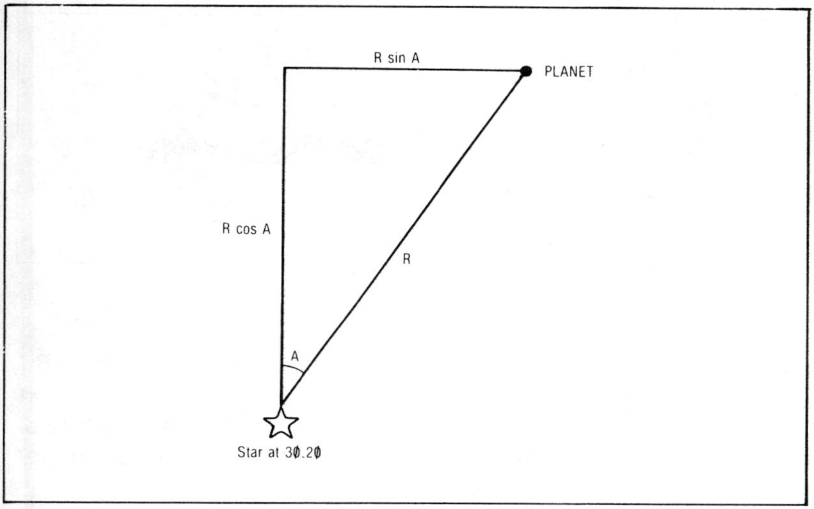

If you delete lines 1ØØ and 11Ø and add these lines:

```
 4Ø FOR A = Ø TO 2 * π STEP .05
13Ø NEXT A
```

your program will draw a circle (of sorts).

DARTING ARROWS

Here is a three-line program that pushes an arrow across the screen:

```
1ØØ FOR J = Ø TO 27
11Ø PRINT AT 15,J;"  ▗";TAB J;""; "▄▄▄▙"TAB J;"   ▞"
12Ø NEXT J
```

The graphics are hard to sort out, but this diagram will help:

PRINT AT 15,J;

TAB J;

TAB J;

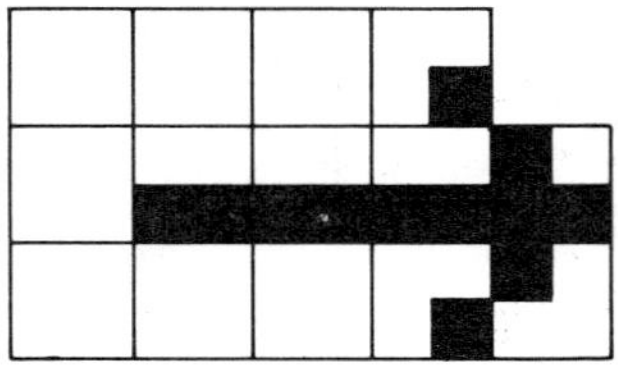

There are two important points here: (1) The technique of using **TAB** J to print an item exactly under a previous item printed at position J on the line. (2) The use of a space at the beginning of the three literal strings which make up the arrow — these automatically erase the remains of previous arrows as we move across the screen.

TRUNDLING TORTOISES

This combines the dice-throwing program from Chapter 25, with the arrow-shooting technique above, to push five tortoises across the screen.

```
 1Ø RAND
 2Ø DIM D(5)
1ØØ CLS
11Ø PRINT "ZX81 TORTOISE RACE"
2ØØ LET T = INT (RND * 5 + 1)
21Ø LET D(T) = D(T) + 1
31Ø PRINT AT T * 3,D(T);" ▄▄▄ "; TAB D(T);" ▗█ ";T;" █▚";
    TAB D(T);" ▘▝"
32Ø IF D(T) < 27 THEN GOTO 2ØØ
4ØØ PRINT AT 21,2Ø;"NO. ";T;"WINS"
41Ø INPUT A$
42Ø RUN
```

A tortoise is printed and moved across just like the arrow (but not quite so fast). This diagram will make the graphics clearer:

PRINT AT T * 3,D(T)

TAB D(T)

TAB D(T)

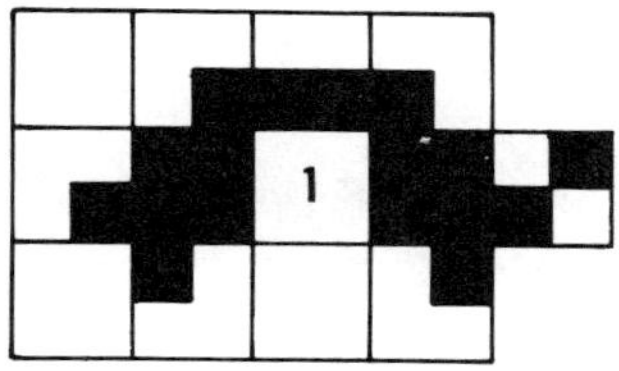

Notice how the tails leave a trail of dashes as the tortoises move. If you don't like this, you will have to include a space just ahead of the tail, and shorten the race by one character.

Perhaps you would like to try your own hand at some graphics problems.

EXERCISE 28.1. FLASHER

Write a subroutine to reward the winner of one of your games — flash the "WINNER" at the bottom right of the screen ten times, leaving it switched on at the end.

EXERCISE 28.2. RUBBER BALL

We saw a program for an everlastingly bouncing ball. Now write a program for a real ball, bouncing vertically, the bounces gradually getting smaller, and finally coming to rest on the floor. This is a hard one — you will need an inner loop to bounce the ball up and down within certain limits, and an outer loop to gradually reduce the upper limit and make the bounces smaller.

EXERCISE 28.3. LUNAR MODULE

We made arrows and tortoises move across the screen. Your problem is to design a little moon-landing module — use any of the characters you like — and move it down the screen onto the moon's surface. It will look better if it is seen to decelerate as it descends!

CHAPTER 29
What a Memory!

BINARY ARITHMETIC

We all know that computers work in binary (base 2) arithmetic. Like most microcomputers, the ZX81 contains a large number of memory cells or *bytes,* each containing an 8-bit number. Here's how to make a working model byte:

Cut a post card in half, longways, mark it out like this and cut along the dashed lines:

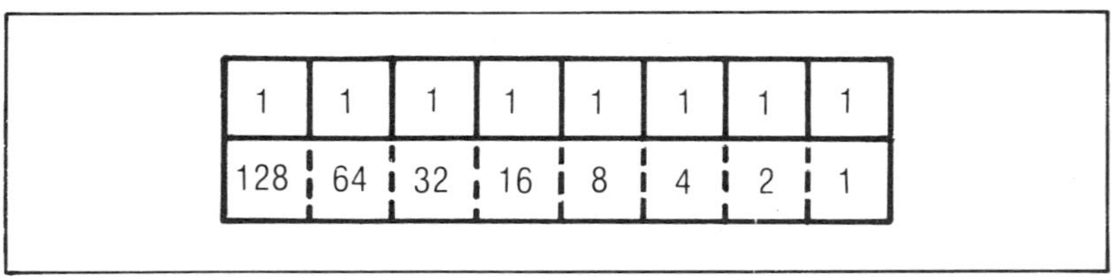

Now fold up all the eight tabs to cover the 1s, and write 0s on the exposed faces like this:

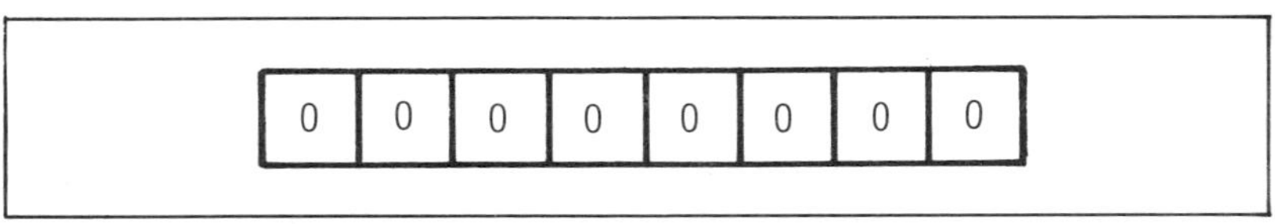

Each bit in your byte can now have the value 0 (folded up) or 1 (hanging down). The decimal value of the number in the byte is found by adding the decimal numbers hanging down:

0	1	0	0	1	1	0	1
	64			8	4		1

Here the binary number in the byte is 01001101, equal to the decimal number 64 + 8 + 4 + 1 = 77.

The smallest decimal number in a byte is of course 0 (all folded up) and the largest is 255 (all hanging down). So the memory cells of the ZX81 are full of numbers between 0 and 255, and these may represent numbers, characters, instructions, and so on. Numbers larger than 255 have to go into two or more bytes, and when we define a variable by:

LET A = 1

the ZX81 sets aside five bytes to contain all possible information on A (size, position of decimal point, sign) plus whatever bytes are needed for the variable name.

ZX81 MEMORIES

The ZX81 memory comes in two parts. The ROM (read only memory) consists of 8K bytes (1K = 2^{10} = 1024 bytes), which contain all the fixed instructions needed to convert BASIC into binary code, and to tell the ZX81 what to do at all times. ROM is permanent, you can find out what is in any byte of ROM but you cannot change it.

The second part is called RAM (random access memory), which consists of 1K byte (1024 bytes numbered from 16384 to 17407). RAM contains all the items which change from program to program — the system variables, your actual program, the display file, and the number and string variables. You can find out the contents of any RAM byte, and you can also change it.

To make full use of your ZX81 you will need the 16K RAM pack. This is a box the size of a pack of cigarettes which clips onto the edge connector at the back of the ZX81. This increases your RAM to a total of 16K or 16383 bytes.

WHAT'S IN THAT BYTE?

To find the contents of a byte of ROM or RAM which has the address number n, we use the function PEEK n. Here is an example:

```
100 LET F = PEEK 16396 + 256 * PEEK 16397
110 PRINT "DISPLAY FILE STARTS","AT BYTE";F
```

What is happening? Well, the first slice of RAM contains the system variables — it is always a fixed size from 16384 up to 16509. The next slice contains your program, which of course can vary in size, followed immediately by the display file (the record of what will be printed on the screen when the program stops). One of the system variables is the starting address of the display file — the ZX81 needs to know this. Being a five-digit number it is contained in two bytes, 16396 and 16397.

Run the program, note the start of the display file, and then add another line of program, say:

```
120 PRINT
```

If you now run again, you will find that the display file has moved along six bytes, the amount of space needed for the new program line. Now, let's find out what is actually in the first ten bytes of the display file.

```
130 FOR J = 0 TO 9
140 PRINT PEEK F + J
150 NEXT J
```

Well, I did warn you that bytes of ROM and RAM simply contain numbers up to 255! Who can remember the function to turn codes into characters? Well done!

```
140 PRINT CHR$ PEEK (F + J)
```

I did say that we could change the contents of any byte of RAM — it is not to be recommended unless you are sure you know what you are doing. The statement is:

POKE m,n
m is the address of the byte we are changing
n is the new value we are putting in (between 0 and 255 of course).
Let's poke an asterisk (code 23) into the top line of the screen display:

```
125 POKE F + 5,23
```

Run the program again and make sure that it worked. You are well on the way to finding out how the ZX81 organizes its memory!

ADVANCED PROGRAMMING

You can write good BASIC programs without ever using a **PEEK** or a **POKE**, but eventually you will find that they let you do things which are otherwise impossible. You will also want to use the **USR** function to write machine code routines — they run faster and use less memory than BASIC. You will need to read your ZX81 operating manual very carefully (Chapters 25 to 28), and buy a more advanced book on programming. Good luck!

WE LEARNED THESE IN CHAPTER 29

STATEMENTS

POKE m,n to put the value n into the byte at address m.

FUNCTIONS

PEEK m gives the contents of byte m as a decimal number.

ANYTHING ELSE

ZX81 memory, 8K of ROM, 1K of RAM plus plug-in expansion to give 16K total RAM.

CHAPTER 30
Debugging Your Programs

You are doing well if you can write a program of any length which runs properly the first time. You are more likely to find that there are errors or "bugs" to be removed.

SYNTAX ERRORS

Generally the ZX81 will not allow this kind of mistake. Leave out a quote or a parenthesis, mix up string and number variables, or commit any other sin in syntax, and the ZX81 will put up the [S] cursor and stop the line from being entered. Make sure your lines do enter, by the way, since you can waste a lot of time typing a new line onto the end of one with a syntax error.

ERRORS WHICH STOP THE PROGRAM

Even if every line has entered correctly, the program may stop running because of some other error. Here the ZX81 helps by printing a report code showing the line number and the type of error that caused the crash. These codes are all listed in Appendix B of your ZX81 operating manual, and often it is obvious what must be done to put things right. Here are a few where the remedy is not quite so obvious.

CODE 2/N. UNDEFINED VARIABLE

All variables must be defined by one of these statements:

LET **INPUT** **FOR** (loop control variables) **DIM** (arrays)

CODE 4/N. NO MORE ROOM IN MEMORY

Common mishap with 1K of RAM which does not go very far, especially if you are using graphics and arrays. Here are some ideas for saving memory, remembering that your RAM is used up by your program and also by your variables and display file.

(1) Cut down the number of variables. Shorten arrays, cut out surplus dummy variables, use the same name for more than one variable in different parts of the program if possible.
(2) Shorten literal strings and string variables, use abbreviations.
(3) Remove **REM** lines.
(4) Look out for duplicated operations — put them into loops or subroutines.
(5) Reduce the amount of screen used for printed output and graphics display.
(6) Consider splitting the program — remember that variables generated in one part can be used in another part.
(7) Start saving for your 16K RAM pack!

CODE 5/N. SCREEN FULL

CONT clears the screen and lets your program continue. In the long run, you'll have to tidy things up by reducing the output, or inserting a pause followed by **CLS**, or using **SCROLL**.

ERRORS WHICH DO NOT STOP THE PROGRAM

Programs often appear to run successfully, but print out rubbish. Remember the old saying that there are no bad computers, only bad programs. Sometimes it's clear that an output is not sensible, at other times, it's not so obvious and you must check carefully. Here are some ideas:

(1) Check your program by putting in data with a known answer.
(2) Check your answer with a hand calculator.
(3) Look for punctuation errors when you are having trouble with tables of results or graphics.
(4) Try out conditional statements by putting in data that does, then does not, satisfy the condition.

(5) Follow the course of your loops (especially nested loops) carefully, preferably using a flowchart.
(6) Put in temporary **PRINT** lines to print the value of your variables at different points in the program.
(7) Break up your program with temporary **STOP** lines and check the different parts separately. Use command **PRINT** to look at your variables, then **CONT** to go on with the program.
(8) It may be useful to use **CLEAR**, as command or statement, to delete all variables before putting in new values of your choice.
(9) Check later parts of your program by using **RUN** n or **GOTO** n to start running your program at line n. Remember that **RUN** clears all variables, **GOTO** does not.

APPENDIX 1

ZX81 BASIC in 8K ROM

A complete list of all the instructions in BASIC available from the ZX81 keyboard.

s	represents a literal string within quotes, or a string variable.
n, m, p	represent numbers, variables or expressions. Where whole numbers are required for n, m, p (as in **PLOT** n,m) the ZX81 rounds off to the nearest whole number (e.g., 10.4 rounded to 10, 10.6 to 11, and 10.5 to 11).

COMMANDS USED IN WRITING AND EDITING PROGRAMS

EDIT	brings a line (indicated by the current line pointer) to the bottom of the screen for editing, and deletes anything already on the bottom of the screen.
⇧ ⇩	moves the current line pointer one line up or down.
⇦ ⇨	moves the cursor one character to the left or right, without affecting text.
FUNCTION	changes the cursor to [F]. The next key pressed puts the corresponding function on the screen and returns the cursor to [L].

GRAPHICS changes the cursor to [G], to obtain graphic blocks and inverses of letters, numbers and some other characters, for use in strings. Press **GRAPHICS** again to return cursor to [L].

LIST displays as much program as possible starting with the first line, and puts the current line pointer above the first line.

LIST n displays as much program as possible starting with line n and puts the current line pointer at line n.

ENTER
(1) transfers a numbered and valid line from the bottom of the screen into the program.
(2) makes the ZX81 execute any command typed on the bottom of the screen.
(3) clears the screen after a run and restores previous listing of program.

DELETE deletes the character or keyword to the left of the cursor.

SHIFT pressing **SHIFT** plus any other key returns the character printed on that key in red.

SYSTEM COMMANDS

Keyword instructions which are not part of the program, but are keyed in and executed once with **ENTER**. ZX81 accepts any keyword as a command, but **INPUT** gives an error Ø/8 and some others don't often make sense. All commands except **BREAK, STOP**, and **COPY** clear the screen before they are executed.

BREAK
(1) stops the ZX81 while it is working. Report code shows where the program stopped, and any output is displayed.
(2) stops the ZX81 during **LOAD** or **SAVE**.

CLEAR deletes all variables.

CONT restarts a program after **BREAK**, **STOP**, or a screen full error.

FAST changes the ZX81 to **FAST** mode (4 × **SLOW**) in which the screen is blank while the screen is working. This is the only mode possible with ZX80.

GOTO n starts running the program at line n, without deleting any variables.

LET defines a variable.

LOAD s sends a program titled s from tape into ZX81 memory, deleting any existing program.

NEW deletes the existing program plus variables in ZX81 memory.

POKE m,n puts the value n (0 to 255) into the memory address m.

PRINT prints on the screen whatever follows the **PRINT** command.

RUN deletes all variables and starts the program at the first line.

RUN n deletes all variables and starts the program at line n.

SAVE s sends a program titled s from the ZX81 memory onto tape for long term storage.

SLOW changes the ZX81 from **FAST** mode to **SLOW**, in which the ZX81 displays all its output while it is working. This is the mode obtained when the ZX81 is switched on, but is not possible on the ZX80.

STOP gets the ZX81 out of an **INPUT** loop when typed as **INPUT**. Quotes must be rubbed out first in a string **INPUT** loop.

PROGRAM STATEMENTS

Keyword instructions which form part of the program. Although the ZX81 will accept any keyword in this way, **CONT** and **NEW** do not often make sense.

CLEAR	deletes all variables.
CLS	clears the screen.
DIM A(n)	sets up a single-dimension numeric array A(1), A(2), . . . A(n) and sets each member to 0.
DIM A(n_1, n_2, . . . n_k)	sets up a multidimension numeric array and sets each member to 0.
DIM B$ (n,m)	sets up a single-dimension array of strings, each having a maximum of m characters, B$(1), B$(2), . . . B$(n) and sets each member to a string of m spaces.
DIM B$ (n_1, n_2, . . . n_k, m)	sets up a multidimension array of strings containing a maximum of m characters each, and sets each member to a string of m spaces.
FAST	changes the ZX81 to **FAST** mode (see command **FAST**).
FOR J = n **TO** m **NEXT** J	sets up a **FOR . . . NEXT** loop. J is set initially at n, and increased by 1 after each circuit. When J > m the loop is ended and the main program continues. The loop is entered n − m + 1 times (once only if m < n), and the final value of J is m + 1.
FOR J = n **TO** m **STEP** p	modifies the **FOR** . . . **NEXT** loop so that J is increased by p after each circuit. If required p may be negative, with m < n.
GOSUB n	jumps to a subroutine at line n, continues from there until **RETURN** is reached, then jumps back to the line following **GOSUB** n.
GOTO n	jumps to line n of the program and continues from there.

IF condition/ **THEN** statement	conditional statement, **IF** the condition is met **THEN** the statement (any keyword) is executed. If the condition is not met, the program continues at the line following.
INPUT	stops the program so that the user can input a value to a numeric or string variable.
LET	assigns a value to a numeric or a string variable.
PAUSE n	stops the program and displays any output for n/60 seconds, or until any key is pressed. If n > 32767, the pause lasts indefinitely until any key is pressed.
PLOT m,n	Blacks in a single pixel (¼ character) on the screen at the position "m along and n up". m = 0 to 63 and n = 0 to 43 inclusive. The next **PRINT** position is immediately after this pixel.
POKE m,n	puts the value n (0 to 255) into the memory address m.
PRINT	prints whatever follows **PRINT** (number, numeric or string variable, expression, literal string) at the current **PRINT** position on the screen.
PRINT AT m,n;	prints whatever follows **PRINT**, at a position m lines down and n characters along, regardless of the current **PRINT** position.
PRINT TAB n;	moves the **PRINT** position to the n th character on the current line (or on the next line if the present **PRINT** position > n), and whatever follows **PRINT** is printed there.
PRINT s (m **TO** n)	prints part of the string s, from the m th to the n th character. If m or n is omitted, then the first or last character is assumed.
RAND	sets a random number as a seed for future **RND** expressions.

REM	indicates a remark, to be ignored by the ZX81.
RETURN	see **GOSUB.**
RUN and **RUN** n	deletes all variables and restarts the program at the beginning or at line n.
SCROLL	moves the screen contents up one line, and sets the **PRINT** position at the beginning of the bottom line.
STEP	see **FOR** . . . **NEXT** . . . **STEP**
SLOW	changes the ZX81 to **SLOW** mode (see command **SLOW**).
STOP	stops the program, and any output up to that point is displayed. Command **CONT** restarts program.
UNPLOT m,n	exactly like **PLOT**, except that **UNPLOT** un-blacks a single pixel on the screen.

COMMANDS/STATEMENTS FOR USE WITH PRINTER

COPY	prints a copy of the screen display.
LLIST	prints a list of the current program.
LLIST n	prints a list of the current program, starting at line n.
LPRINT	prints whatever follows **LPRINT.**

NUMERIC FUNCTIONS

ABS n	the absolute value of n (with sign removed).
ARCCOS n	the angle (in radians) which has the cosine n.
ARCSIN n	the angle (in radians) which has the sine n.
ARCTAN n	the angle (in radians) which has the tangent n.
COS n	the cosine of n (angle in radians).
EXP n	e^n (the natural antilog of n).
INT n	the integer part of n.
LN n	the natural log of n (base e).

PEEK n	the value currently stored at memory address n.
PI (or π)	3.14159 . . .
RND	a pseudo-random number between 0 and 1.
SGN n	the sign portion of n. If n positive **SGN** n = 1, if n = 0 **SGN** n = 0, if n negative **SGN** n = −1.
SIN n	the sine of n (angle in radians).
SQR n	the square root of n.
TAN n	the tangent of n (angle in radians).
USR n	calls the machine code subroutine at address n.

STRING-HANDLING FUNCTIONS

CHR$ n	the character which has the code n (n between 0 and 255 inclusive).
CODE s	the code number of the first character of s.
INKEY$	reads the whole keyboard. **INKEY$** is a single character corresponding to a key pressed, or the null string if no key is pressed.
LEN s	the length (number of characters) of the string s.
STR$ n	converts the number n to an apparently identical string "n".
VAL s	converts the string s, if possible, to a number or an expression which is evaluated as a number.

LOGICAL OPERATORS

NOT **AND** **OR**	used with **IF** in conditional statements.

ARITHMETIC OPERATORS

n**m	n raised to the power of m.
−n	negatives the value of n.
n*m	n times m.
n/m	n divided by m.
n + m	n plus m.
n − m	n minus m.

RELATIONAL OPERATORS

Used to compare two numbers, variables or expressions. = is also used with **LET** to assign a value to a variable.

n = m	n equals m.
n < m	n is less than m.
n > m	n is greater than m.
n < = m	n is less than or equal to m.
n > = m	n is greater than or equal to m.
n <> m	n is not equal to m.

NOT can be used with any of these, e.g., **NOT** n = m is the same as n <> m.

PUNCTUATION

;	instruction to print the next **PRINT** item immediately following the item before;
,	instruction to move to the beginning of the next **PRINT** zone, and print the next item there. Each line on the screen is divided into two equal **PRINT** zones.
"	marks the beginning and end of a literal string or a string **INPUT**, or for defining a string variable.
	used as a decimal point.
"" ""	a picture of a quotation mark for use inside strings.

( )	used to change the priority in a numerical expression or a logical statement.

With the exception of '' all the above (as well as : and ?) may be used inside strings.

APPENDIX 2

Glossary of Terms

Address The number which identifies a byte of memory.

Back up storage Some method of long term storage of programs and variables, e.g., a cassette recorder.

BASIC Originally designed for beginners, now one of the most widely used high level languages for microcomputers.

Binary digit (Bit) One digit from a binary number; can only be 0 or 1.

Binary number A number in the binary system (base 2), where all the digits are 0 or 1, instead of 0 to 9 as in the decimal (base 10) system.

Bug An error in a program which prevents it from doing what is required of it.

Byte A binary number 8 bits long, the normal storage unit in a microcomputer memory.

Character Any item which can be stored in one byte and printed on the screen, e.g., A 1 ; PRINT are all ZX81 characters.

Character codes The single byte number which identifies each character — these may vary from one computer to another.

Command An instruction which does not form part of the program, but which makes the computer take action of some kind.

Concatenation Joining two or more strings together like links in a chain.

Conditional statement A statement which is carried out only if a given condition is satisfied.

Crash The program stops running because of a program or data error.

Debug To find and remove errors from a program.

Edit To select and alter any chosen line in a program.

Enter To transfer a program line, or a command, or some data from the keyboard to the computer (by pressing **ENTER** on the ZX81).

Empty string A string containing no characters at all (also called a null string).

Firmware Sometimes used to denote the interpeter program, and other permanent programs found in ROM.

Flowchart A representation in diagrammatic form of a series of connected operations to be done in a specified sequence.

Function Some specified operation which is carried out on the number or string which follows.

Hardware The physical parts of a computer and the surrounding equipment, as opposed to programs.

High-level language Programming language made up of a set of recognizable English words.

Integer A whole number which may be positive or negative.

K (of memory) A unit of memory containing 1024 bytes.

Keyword A command, statement or function occupying one byte of memory and entered by one or two keystrokes.

Literal string A set of characters enclosed by quotation marks and printed literally on the screen by the computer.

Load To transfer a program from back up storage to the computer.

Loop Part of a program which is carried out repeatedly.

Low-level language Programming language which uses machine code.

Machine code Programming code which uses the hexadecimal system to represent binary numbers.

Nested loops Loops within loops, so that the instructions in inner loops are carried out several times for each pass around the outer loop.

Null string See *Empty string.*

Numeric array A set of numeric variables each identified by an array name and subscript number(s).

Numerical variable A variable with some given name, to which can be assigned any desired number value or numerical expression.

Pixel Short for picture cell. The smallest graphics unit which can be printed on the screen. In the ZX81 system the screen is filled by 63 pixels across and 43 pixels up.

Printer Connected to a computer to allow it to produce its output in permanent form on paper.

Priority The order in which arithmetical or logical operations are carried out.

Program A numbered list of instructions to be carried out by a computer.

Pseudo-random numbers These have an apparently random distribution but each number is in fact calculated by the computer from the previous number, and they are therefore not truly random.

Random access memory (RAM) Computer memory used by the programmer for storage of programs, data, and so on. Each byte of RAM can be read or altered at will.

Random number A number drawn from a given set, where each number in the set is equally likely to be drawn and the draw is not affected by previous events.

Read only memory (ROM) Permanent computer memory generally used to contain BASIC interpreter programs, operating systems and so on. Can be read but not changed.

Relational operators Symbols like =, <, >, used to compare numbers, expressions or strings

Report code A signal from the ZX81 which is shown at the end of a successful run, or when the program is stopped by **BREAK, STOP** or an error.

Save To transfer a program into back up storage for use.

Scientific notation In which a number is displayed in terms of its mantissa (a number between 0 and 10) and its exponent (the power of ten by which the mantissa is to be multiplied). The ZX81 uses this system for very large or very small numbers, which it would not have room to display otherwise.

Software Computer programs and manuals, as opposed to hardware.

Statement An instruction to the computer which forms part of the program.

String array A set of string variables identified by an array name and subscript number(s). In ZX81 BASIC, a string array contains one extra final dimension showing the length of each member.

String variable A variable, identified in BASIC by a name ending in the $ sign, to which may be assigned a string of characters of any kind (with minor exceptions).

Subroutine A part of the program to which the computer can be directed from any part of the main program. When the subroutine has been carried out, the computer is directed back to the line following its original departure point.

Syntax error Some error in the structure of a program line which prevents it from being executed, and in the case of the ZX81, from being entered into the program.

APPENDIX 3
Programs for the ZX81

This appendix contains 14 programs that can be run on your ZX81. The names of these programs are as follows:

1. Random rectangles (1K)
2. Square spiral (1K)
3. Random bar chart (1K)
4. Sales chart (1K)
5. Moving average (1K)
6. Multiples (1K)
7. Finding factors of numbers (1K)
8. Number base conversion (1K)
9. Drawing pictures (1K)
   Drawing pictures and storing them in an array (16K)
10. Cows and bulls (1K)
11. Electronic dice (1K)
12. Reaction timer (1K)
13. Black box (16K)
14. Telephone list (16K)

1. RANDOM RECTANGLES (1K)

The program uses part of the screen (about ⅔) in which to draw an unlimited series of rectangles of random size and at random positions.

```
 10 RAND
100 LET A = INT (RND*44)
110 LET B = INT (RND*44)
120 LET C = INT (RND*44)
130 LET D = INT (RND*44)
140 IF A = C THEN LET A = A + 1
150 IF B = D THEN LET B = B + 1
200 FOR J = A TO C STEP SIGN (C − A)
210 PLOT J,B
220 PLOT J,D
230 NEXT J
240 FOR J = B TO D STEP SGN (D − B)
250 PLOT A,J
260 PLOT C,J
270 NEXT J
300 GOTO 100
```

LIST OF VARIABLES

A, B	coordinates of one corner of a rectangle.
C, D	coordinates of the opposite corner.
J	loop control variable.

NOTES

Lines 100 to 150	set the corner coordinates to random 0 to 43, and make sure that A and C, B and D are not equal.
Lines 200 to 230	draw the horizontal sides. A may be larger or smaller than C, so we use **STEP SGN** (C − A), which may be +1 or −1, to make sure that the **FOR/NEXT** loop works properly.
Lines 240 to 270	draw the vertical sides.

Line 300 goes back for the next rectangle. We do not need to include **RAND** in the loop — in certain programs this could produce the opposite effect to randomizing.

With 16K of RAM, you can let A and C go up to the full 63 which **PLOT** allows. You can easily change this program to draw a definite number of rectangles, or for use as a subroutine to draw a rectangle, given the coordinates of opposite corners.

2. SQUARE SPIRAL (1K)

A useless but pretty program which alternately draws and then rubs out a square spiral in the middle of the screen. Perhaps you could modify it to draw a rectangular spiral which could be used in a program title.

```
 10 LET S = 1000
 20 LET D = 25
 30 LET H = 5
 40 LET V = 18
 50 LET S = 3000-S
 90 IF D = 1 THEN GOTO 20
100 FOR H = H TO H + D
110 GOSUB S
120 NEXT H
130 LET D = D-1
200 FOR V = V TO V+D
210 GOSUB S
220 NEXT V
230 LET D = D-1
300 FOR H = H TO H-D STEP-1
310 GOSUB S
320 NEXT H
330 LET D = D-1
400 FOR V = V TO V-D STEP-1
410 GOSUB S
420 NEXT V
430 LET D = D-1
440 GOTO 90
```

```
1ØØØ UNPLOT V,H
1Ø1Ø RETURN
2ØØØ PLOT V,H
2Ø1Ø RETURN
```

LIST OF VARIABLES

S	flag to determine which subroutine is entered.
D	width of spiral.
H, V	coordinates of starting point.

NOTES

Line 5Ø	sets the flag S to 2ØØØ or 1ØØØ in alternate passes of the loop.
Line 9Ø	checks for end of main loop, then goes back to reset variables.
Lines 1ØØ to 12Ø	draw the first vertical line.
Line 13Ø	reduces the length of the side by one.
Lines 2ØØ to 23Ø	draw the next horizontal side.
Lines 23Ø to 43Ø	draw the remaining two sides.
Line 44Ø	goes back to line 9Ø to draw the next bit of the spiral.
Lines 1ØØØ to 2ØØØ	alternative subroutines to plot or unplot the spiral.

3. RANDOM BAR CHART (1K)

The program prints a set of fifty vertical bars of random height, and works out and prints the mean height of the fifty bars.

```
 5 LET T = Ø
1Ø FOR J = Ø TO 49
2Ø LET R = INT (RND* 4Ø + 1)
3Ø LET T = T + R
4Ø FOR K = Ø TO R
5Ø PLOT J,K
6Ø NEXT K
```

```
 70 NEXT J
 80 PAUSE 100
 90 FOR J = 0 TO 49
100 PLOT J,T/50
110 NEXT J
120 PRINT TAB 5;"MEAN R = ";T/50
```

LIST OF VARIABLES

T	total of the random numbers.
J,K	loop control variables.
R	a random number between 1 and 40.

NOTES

Lines 10 to 30	this part of the J loop generates fifty random numbers between 1 and 40 and totals them.
Lines 40 to 60	this K loop draws a vertical bar equal in height to the current random number R.
Lines 90 to 110	plot a horizontal line as near as possible to the mean height of the fifty bars.
Line 120	prints the mean of the fifty random numbers.

4. SALES CHART (1K)

A demonstration bar chart showing sales of nuts and bolts during the past five years.

```
 10 DIM S(5,2)
100 FOR J = 1 TO 5
110 FOR K = 1 TO 2
120 LET S(J,K) = INT (RND*11 + 10)
130 NEXT K
140 NEXT J
200 PRINT "FIVE YEAR SALES FIGS", "FOR NUTS ( ) AND
    BOLTS ( )",,,
250 PRINT "YEAR",,
```

```
300 FOR J = 1 TO 5
305 PRINT 1976 + J; " ";
310 FOR K = 1 TO 2Ø
320 IF S(J,1) > = K AND  S(J,2) > = K THEN PRINT "▓";
330 IF S(J,L) > = K AND S(J,2) < K THEN PRINT "▄";
340 IF S(J,2) > = K AND S(J,1) < K THEN PRINT "▀";
350 NEXT K
360 PRINT
370 PRINT
380 NEXT J
4ØØ PRINT"Ø 2 4 6 8 1 1 1 1 1 2"        (4 spaces)
41Ø PRINT"              Ø 2 4 6 8 Ø"    (14 spaces)
```

LIST OF VARIABLES

S(5,2)	5 × 2 array of sales figures for two items during five years.
J,K	loop control variables.

NOTES

Lines 1ØØ to 14Ø	generate a set of random sales figures in the range 1Ø to 2Ø.
Lines 3ØØ, and 36Ø to 38Ø	outside loop, dealing with the five years.
Lines 31Ø to 35Ø	print a bar on the chart for one year, with tests to determine which of the three possible graphic blocks is to be printed.

5. MOVING AVERAGE (1K)

The input to the program consists of a continuous series of figures, for instance monthly sales figures. The program takes the N most recent figures (you specify N), and calculates the mean and standard deviation.

```
 1Ø LET K = Ø
1ØØ PRINT "HOW MANY NOS.?"
11Ø INPUT N
12Ø DIM X(N)
```

```
2ØØ LET K = K + 1
21Ø PRINT "NEXT NUMBER?";
22Ø INPUT X(K)
23Ø PRINT X(K)
24Ø IF K < N THEN GOTO 2ØØ
25Ø CLS
3ØØ LET SX = Ø
31Ø LET SS = Ø
32Ø PRINT "LAST";N;"NUMBERS",,,,
33Ø FOR J = 1 TO N
34Ø LET SX = SX + X(J)
35Ø LET SS = SS + X(J)**2
36Ø PRINT"          ";X(J)
37Ø IF J > 1 THEN LET X(J - 1) = X(J)
38Ø NEXT J
4ØØ PRINT,, "MEAN = ";SX/N
41Ø PRINT,, "STD DEV = ";SQR (SS/N - (SX/N)**2),,,,,
42Ø GOTO 21Ø
```

LIST OF VARIABLES

K	subscript for the X(n) figure currently being input.
N	the number of figures to be averaged at a time.
X(N)	an array of N numbers.
SX	the sum of the last N numbers.
SS	the sum of the squares of the last N numbers.

NOTES

Lines 1ØØ to 12Ø	input the number of figures to be averaged at a time, and dimensions X(N) accordingly.
Lines 2ØØ to 24Ø	**INPUT** loop for X(N). At the beginning, it is entered N times, after that only once for each new calculation.
Lines 33Ø to 38Ø	J loop which takes each of the X(N) numbers in order, and does these four things with them: 1 Sums them (SX). 2 Sums their squares (SS). 3 Prints them. 4 With the exception of X(1), drops each number down one place in the array, so

that X(1) is lost, X(2) becomes X(1), X(3) becomes X(2), and so on.

Lines 400 to 410 — calculate and print the mean and the standard deviation of the last N numbers.

Line 420 — goes back for a new X(N).

Obviously this program can be simplified to calculate the mean and standard deviation of a single set of numbers.

6. MULTIPLES (1K)

The program prints out a 0 to 99 number square, with the multiples of any given number printed in inverse.

```
 10 PRINT "TYPE ANY NUMBER, 0 TO 99"
 20 INPUT N
 30 CLS
100 PRINT "THE MULTIPLES OF ";N;" ARE"
110 IF N = 0 THEN LET N = 100
200 FOR J = 0 TO 9
210 FOR K = 0 TO 9
220 IF J = 0 THEN PRINT " ";
230 LET M = 10*J + K
240 IF INT (M / N)*N = M THEN GOTO 500
250 PRINT M; " ";
260 NEXT K
270 PRINT
280 PRINT
290 NEXT J
300 GOTO 10
500 IF J > 0 THEN PRINT CHR$ (J + 156);
510 PRINT CHR$ (K + 156);" ";
520 GOTO 260
```

LIST OF VARIABLES

N	chosen number for multiples.
J,K	loop control variables.
M	the current number in the number square.

NOTES

Line 110	changes N to 100 if N = 0, to avoid a dividing by zero error in line 240. 0 is always printed in inverse since it is a multiple of every other number.
Line 230	generates the current number in the square from J and K.
Line 240	tests the current number to see if it is a multiple of N.
Line 250	prints nonmultiples normally.
Lines 500 to 510	print multiples of N in inverse by using the fact that the code of an inverse number is 156 more than the actual number.

7. FINDING FACTORS OF NUMBERS (1K)

The first version of this program works by *iteration* — repeating the same operations over and over again. It takes a given number, divides it by two until that "won't go", then divides by three, etc. If there are no factors apart from the number itself, it announces "prime number".

```
100 PRINT "FACTORIZING NUMBERS"
110 PRINT "WHATS YOUR NUMBER"
120 INPUT N
130 LET NN = N
140 LET F = 2
170 PRINT ,,,,N;" = 1";
200 IF N / F <> INT (N / F) THEN GOTO 300
220 PRINT "X";F;
230 LET N = N / F
250 GOTO 200
300 IF N = 1 THEN GOTO 400
330 LET F = F + 1
340 GOTO 200
400 IF F = NN THEN PRINT "PRIME NUMBER"
410 PRINT
420 PRINT,, "THATS ALL"
430 PRINT AT 21,19;"PRESS ENTER"
440 INPUT A$
450 CLS
460 GOTO 100
```

LIST OF VARIABLES

N	number to be factorized.
NN	dummy variable.
F	the factor currently being tried.
A$	input empty string to continue with another number N.

NOTES

Line 130	puts N into a dummy variable NN.
Line 140	sets the factor to 2 to start with.
Line 200	checks whether N is divisible by F.
Lines 230 to 250	N is divisible by F, so N is divided by F, and then sent back to line 200 to try again.
Line 300	checks whether N has been reduced to 1, in which case it is time to stop dividing by F.
Lines 330 to 340	N is not divisible by F, so increase F by 1, then back to line 200 to try again.
Line 400	if N is the same as NN when all possible factors have been tried, N must be a prime number.

The program works well but is desperately slow — try putting in 1998 and then 1997. The reason is that we are trying a whole lot of impossible numbers as factors — for instance we can rule out all the even numbers after 2. Also, if we have a prime number, there is no point in trying to divide by any factor bigger than its square root. So, let's type in some more lines to deal with these two points.

```
150 LET S = SQR N
160 LET PF = 0
200 IF N / F <> INT (N / F) OR NN = 2 THEN GOTO 300
240 LET PF = 1
300 IF PF = 0 AND F > S OR N = 1 THEN GOTO 400
310 IF F = 2 THEN LET F = 1
330 LET F = F + 2
400 IF PF = 0 THEN PRINT "X";NN;"PRIME NUMBER"
```

It's better now, but there's still a long way to go, for instance try putting in 3994 (which is 2 times a large prime). You will learn a lot about programming, and also about numbers, if you try to improve on my effort, using a flowchart.

8. NUMBER BASE CONVERSION (1K)

This program converts numbers from base ten to base two, or vice versa.

```
 10 LET B$ = "BASE 10 NO. ="
 20 LET C$ = "BASE 2 NO. ="
 50 PRINT "NUMBER BASE CONVERSION"
 60 PRINT,, "CHANGING FROM WHICH BASE?", "2 OR 10?"
 70 INPUT T
 80 CLS
 90 IF T = 2 THEN GOTO 600
110 PRINT
120 PRINT,, B$;
130 INPUT T
140 PRINT T,,C$;
160 FOR J = INT (LN T/LN 256*8) TO 0 STEP - 1
170 IF 2**J > T THEN GOTO 210
180 LET T = T - 2**J
190 PRINT "1";
200 GOTO 220
210 PRINT "0" ;
220 NEXT J
230 GOTO 110
600 LET T = 0
610 PRINT
620 PRINT,,C$;
630 INPUT A$
640 PRINT A$
650 FOR J = 0 TO LEN A$ - 1
660 LET T = T + VAL A$ (LEN A$ - J)*2**J
670 NEXT J
680 PRINT B$;T
690 GOTO 600
```

LIST OF VARIABLES

B$, C$	strings used more than once.
T	1 choice of base to convert from.
	2 base 10 number to be converted.
	3 result of converting a base 2 number.
A$	Base 2 number to be converted.

NOTES

Line 9∅	program branches according to choice of base.
Line 16∅	sets the J loop to start at the correct number of places for the base 2 number.
Line 17∅	checks whether the current digit should be 0 or 1.
Lines 18∅ to 19∅	if 1, remove the current power of 2 from T, and print "1".
Line 21∅	otherwise, prints "∅".
Lines 65∅ to 67∅	take the digits of the base 2 number, one by one, multiply them by the current power of 2, and sum them as T.

T has been used for three different variables to save memory — this is allowable because T is redefined in all three places. There are other ways of converting between different number bases. Try to work out other methods, and different bases — hexadecimal is an important one.

9. DRAWING PICTURES (1K AND 16K)

The 1K program will allow you to use about ⅔ of the screen on which to draw pictures, with the drawing pixel under control of the four arrows at 5, 6, 7, 8 on keyboard. If you press D (for draw), the pixel leaves a continuous trail wherever it goes. If you press R (for rubout) it leaves no trail, and erases any previous drawing over which it passes.

```
10 LET X = 0
20 LET Y = 10
30 LET F$ = "R"
```

```
100 IF INKEY$ = "R" THEN LET F$ = INKEY$
110 IF INKEY$ = "D" THEN LET F$ = INKEY$
190 IF F$ = "R" THEN UNPLOT X,Y
200 IF INKEY$ = "5" THEN LET X = X - 1
210 IF INKEY$ = "6" THEN LET Y = Y - 1
220 IF INKEY$ = "7" THEN LET Y = Y + 1
230 IF INKEY$ = "8" THEN LET X = X + 1
300 IF X > 50 THEN LET X = 50
310 IF X < 0 THEN LET X = 0
320 IF Y > 43 THEN LET Y = 43
330 IF Y < 10 THEN LET Y = 10
340 PLOT X,Y
400 GOTO 100
```

LIST OF VARIABLES

X,Y	coordinates of the present PLOT/UNPLOT point.
F$	flag for "draws" or "erase".

NOTES

Lines 100 to 400	main loop in which all inputs are by **INKEY$.**
Lines 100 to 110	set flag F$ for "draw" or "erase".
Line 190	**UNPLOT** activated only in "erase" mode.
Lines 200 to 230	**PLOT** point changed by the four cursor arrow keys.
Lines 300 to 330	keep the **PLOT** position within a fixed rectangle.

In the 16K program the drawing space has been reduced to a smaller rectangle, but otherwise the first part of the program works just as above. When you have completed your drawing, press Z, and the contents of the drawing rectangle are found by **PEEK** and put into an array. Now, by **GOTO** 2000, the drawing is repeated at any desired position on the screen. If desired, the array can be saved with lines 2000 to 2060 for future use.

Type the following lines in addition to those of the 1K program:

```
  40 DIM A(80)
 300 IF X > 19 THEN LET X = 19
 330 IF Y < 28 THEN LET Y = 28
 350 IF INKEY$ = "Z" THEN GOTO 1000
1000 LET F = PEEK 16396 + 256*PEEK 16397
1020 FOR J = 0 TO 7
1030 FOR K = 1 TO 10
1040 LET A(10*J + K) = PEEK (F + K + 33*J)
1050 NEXT K
1060 NEXT J
1070 STOP
2000 PRINT AT 5,10
2010 FOR J = 0 TO 7
2020 FOR K = 1 TO 10
2030 PRINT CHR$ A(10*J + K);
2040 NEXT K
2050 PRINT TAB 10;
2060 NEXT J
```

LIST OF VARIABLES

F	the byte which starts the display file.
J,K	loop control variables.
A(80)	the set of code numbers representing the contents of the drawing space.

NOTES

Line 350	sets flag to leave the main loop.
Line 1000	finds the start of the display file.
Lines 1020 to 1060	determine the code numbers corresponding to the contents of the drawing rectangle, and put them into the array A(80).
Line 2000, line 2050	set the new printing position for the picture.
Line 2010 to 2060	repeat the contents of the drawing rectangle in the new position.

10. COWS AND BULLS (1K)

A simple version of the old game, started in Exercise 25.1. The ZX81 generates a four digit number — digits between 1 and 6, and may be the same — and you have nine tries to guess it. After each guess, black blobs tell you the number of bulls scored (right digit in the right position), and gray blobs the number of cows (right digit but wrong position).

```
  20 DIM N(4)
 100 FOR J = 1 TO 4
 110 LET N(J) = INT (RND*6 + 1)
 120 NEXT J
 200 FOR X = 1 TO 9
 210 PRINT "GUESS NO"; X;"?";
 220 INPUT G$
 230 PRINT G$
 300 FOR J = 1 TO 4
 310 IF G$(J) = STR$ N(J) THEN GOSUB 1000
 320 NEXT J
 330 FOR J = 1 TO 4
 340 FOR K = 1 TO 4
 350 IF G$(K) = STR$ N(J) THEN GOSUB 1100
 360 NEXT K
 370 LET N(J) = ABS N(J)
 380 NEXT J
 390 PRINT
 400 NEXT X
 900 STOP
1000 PRINT "█";
1010 LET G$(J) = " "
1020 GOTO 1120
1100 PRINT "▒";
1110 LET G$(K) = " "
1120 LET N(J) = -N(J)
1130 RETURN
```

LIST OF VARIABLES

N(4)	four random digits between 1 and 6.
X,J,K	loop control variables.
G$	player's current guess at the hidden number.

NOTES

Lines 100 to 120	generate the hidden four digit number.
Lines 300 to 320	test the four digits of the current guess for bulls.
Lines 330 to 380	test as above for cows.
Line 370	restores the digits of the hidden number ready for the next guess.
Lines 1000 to 1130	subroutine dealing with cow and bull scoring. It is entered at different points for cow or bull score, but there is a common ending and return.
Lines 1010 and 1110	cancel the current digit of the guess, when it has resulted in a cow or bull score.
Line 1120	cancels the current digit of the hidden number when it has been the subject of a cow or bull score.

11. ELECTRONIC DICE (1K)

This program generates pseudo-random numbers from 1 to 6, and converts them into pictures of an actual dice face.

```
  10 RAND
 100 FOR J = 1 TO 9
 120 PRINT AT J + 6,10; "█████████"      (9 inverse spaces)
 140 NEXT J
 200 LET D = INT (RND*6 + 1)
 210 GOSUB 1000 + D*100
 220 INPUT A$
 230 CLS
 240 GOTO 100
1100 PRINT AT 11,14;" "       (1 space)
1110 IF D = 1 THEN RETURN
1200 PRINT AT 8,11; " "       (1 space)
1210 PRINT AT 14,17; " "      (1 space)
1220 RETURN
1300 GOTO 1100
1400 PRINT AT 8,11; " █████ "      (1 space, 5 inverse spaces,
     1 space)
```

1410 **PRINT AT** 14,11; "   "   (as 1400)
1420 **RETURN**
1500 **PRINT AT** 11,14;" "   (1 space)
1510 **GOTO** 1400
1600 **PRINT AT** 8,11; "   "   (1 space, 2 inverse spaces, 1 space, 2 inverse spaces, 1 space)
1610 **PRINT AT** 14, 11; "   "   (as 1600)
1620 **RETURN**

LIST OF VARIABLES

J	loop control variable.
D	pseudo-random number between 1 and 6.
A$	empty string input to throw the dice again.

NOTES

Lines 100 to 140	draw the dice square.
Lines 200 to 210	generate a random number D, and direct the ZX81 to the corresponding subroutine.
Lines 1100 to 1620	six subroutines for printing spots on the dice. Rather an untidy lot of **GOTO**s and **RETURN**s, but it is meant to minimize the use of RAM.

12. REACTION TIMER (1K)

Follow the instructions, and this program will measure your reaction time and print it on a scale running from 0 to 60. The absolute accuracy is not very high, but it is consistent!

---

90 **PRINT AT** 0, 0;" HOW FAST DO YOU REACT?   "
100 **PRINT** " PRESS ANY KEY   "
110 **PRINT** " WHEN THE SCREEN CLEARS "
(three lines above use inverse spaces and letters)
160 **PRINT AT** 11,1;
170 **FAST**

```
190 PAUSE RND*3ØØ+2ØØ
21Ø FOR A = Ø TO 62
22Ø IF INKEY$ <>" "THEN GOTO 47Ø
23Ø PRINT" █ ";        (graphic block SHIFT 5)
24Ø PRINT" ";          (empty string)
25Ø NEXT A
46Ø IF A = 63 THEN PRINT "SLOW" (inverse letters)
47Ø IF A = Ø THEN PRINT "CHEAT"
475 SLOW
49Ø PRINT
5ØØ FOR J = Ø TO 12
51Ø PRINT TAB J*5;J*5;
52Ø NEXT J
53Ø PRINT TAB 9;"MILLISECS"
54Ø PRINT,, TAB 5;"25 IS ABOUT AVERAGE"
55Ø PAUSE 2ØØ
56Ø CLS
57Ø GOTO 1Ø
```

LIST OF VARIABLES

A,J	loop control variables.

NOTES

Lines 9Ø to 11Ø	print a bold black heading.
Lines 17Ø to 19Ø	sets **FAST** mode, then after a random pause, the screen clears (ZX81 working in fast mode).
Lines 22Ø to 25Ø	timing loop, taking about 1 millisecond per pass. Line 22Ø jumps out of the timing loop when any key is pressed.
Line 47Ø	checks for cheating — key pressed before start of timing loop.
Lines 475 to 54Ø	back into **SLOW** mode and print scale.

13. BLACK BOX (16K)

Waddingtons produce an excellent board game called *Black Box,* and here is a version of this for the ZX81. The board consists of an eight by eight square, numbered from 1 to 32 around the perimeter. Four atoms are hidden inside the square, and you have to find them by shooting laser beams into the box from the various numbered positions. If you hit an atom, the beam is absorbed (shown by *). If there is an atom in the line next to your beam, the beam bounces off of it, and eventually emerges from the box as shown by flashing letters. In the absence of atoms in its vicinity, the beam goes straight through the box. Warning — the beam can bounce off of more than one atom in its passage through the box. If the beam finds atoms in the lines on both sides of the beam it is reflected straight back (shown by ▧). A reflection is also shown if there is an atom at the edge of the board next to your entry point.

You can guess where the atoms are, one by one, but be careful — there is a three shot penalty for a wrong guess. If you give up, the ZX81 will show you where the atoms were.

The rules are hard to explain, but you'll catch on to them quickly. This is an original program — there are other versions around but I venture to hope that my graphics are better than most.

```
  5 RAND
 10 DIM A(10,10)
 20 LET S = 37
 30 LET B$ = "         " (9 spaces)
 40 LET NS = 0
 50 LET RG = 0
100 FOR J = 0 TO 11
110 PRINT AT J + 5,9; "████████████" (12 inverse spaces)
120 NEXT J
130 PRINT AT 10,10;"BLACK BOX"        (inverse letters)
180 PRINT AT 21,20;"PLEASE WAIT"
190 PAUSE 200
200 FAST
205 CLS
210 GOSUB 1000
215 SLOW
220 GOSUB 1200
230 GOSUB 3300
250 PRINT AT 0,22;"WHAT NOW?";TAB 23;" ";TAB 23; """"S""
    = SHOOT"; TAB 23; " "; TAB 23; """"G"" = GUESS"; TAB
    24;" ";TAB 24;" ";TAB 24;""""E"" = END"
```

```
270 GOSUB 4200
280 GOSUB 3300
285 IF I$ = "G" THEN GOTO 3600
290 IF I$ = "S" THEN GOTO 305
295 IF I$ = "E" THEN GOTO 1300
305 LET NS = NS + 1
310 PRINT AT 10,25; "SHOT";TAB 26;"NO."; NS
420 LET S = S + 1
430 LET S$ = CHR$ S
490 PRINT AT 0,21;"WHAT NUMBER";TAB 23;"ARE YOU";
    TAB 24;"SHOOTING";TAB 26; "FROM?"
500 INPUT N
510 IF N < 9 THEN GOSUB 1400
520 IF N > 8 AND N < 17 THEN GOSUB 2300
530 IF N > 16 AND N < 25 THEN GOSUB 2000
540 IF N > 24 AND N < 33 THEN GOSUB 1700
550 IF N > 32 THEN GOTO 500
560 GOTO 240
990 STOP
1000 REM**DRAWING THE BOX
1010 PRINT AT 3,0;
1020 FOR J = 1 TO 16
1030 PRINT "   ████████████████" (3 spaces, 16 inverse spaces)
1040 NEXT J
1060 FOR J = 1 TO 8
1070 PRINT AT 0,2 + 2*J; J
1080 PRINT AT 1 + 2*J,21;J + 8
1090 PRINT AT 20,4;"2 2 2 2 2 1 1 1"
1095 PRINT AT 21,4;"4 3 2 1 0 9 8 7"
1100 PRINT AT 19 - 2*J,0;J + 24
1110 NEXT J
1120 FOR J = 6 TO 38 STEP 4
1130 FOR K = 6 TO 38
1140 UNPLOT J,K
1150 UNPLOT K,J
1160 NEXT K
1170 NEXT J
1180 RETURN
1200 REM**PLACING FOUR ATOMS
1210 FOR J = 1 TO 4
1220 LET X = INT (RND*8 + 2)
1230 LET Y = INT (RND*8 + 2)
```

```
1240 IF A(X,Y) = 1 THEN GOTO 1220
1250 LET A(X,Y) = 1
1260 NEXT J
1270 RETURN
1300 REM**PRINTING 4 ATOMS
1310 FOR X = 2 TO 9
1320 FOR Y = 2 TO 9
1330 IF A(X, Y) = 1 THEN PRINT AT 21 - 2*Y,2*X;"*"
     (inverse *)
1340 NEXT Y
1350 NEXT X
1360 GOTO 3900
1400 REM**MOVING SOUTH
1410 LET X = N + 1
1420 LET Y = 10
1430 LET L = 2
1440 LET C = 2 + 2*(X - 1)
1450 PRINT AT L, C;S$
1460 FOR J = 1 TO 30
1470 NEXT J
1475 IF A(X,9) = 1 THEN GOTO 3000
1480 IF A(X - 1, Y - 1) = 1 OR A(X + 1, Y - 1) = 1 THEN GOTO
     2600
1490 IF A(X + 1, Y - 1) = 1 AND A(X - 1, Y - 1) = 1 THEN
     GOTO 2600
1500 IF A (X + 1, Y - 1) = 1 THEN GOTO 2390
1510 IF A(X - 1, Y - 1) = 1 THEN GOTO 1790
1520 IF A(X, Y - 1) = 1 THEN GOTO 3000
1530 IF Y = 2 THEN GOTO 1560
1540 LET Y = Y - 1
1550 GOTO 1490
1560 LET L1 = 19
1570 LET C1 = 2 + 2*(X - 1)
1580 GOTO 4000
1700 REM**MOVING EAST
1710 LET X = 1
1720 LET Y = N - 23
1730 LET L = 19 - 2*(Y - 1)
1740 LET C = 2
1750 PRINT AT  L,C;S$
1760 FOR J = 1 TO 30
1770 NEXT J
```

```
1775 IF A(2, Y) = 1 THEN GOTO 3000
1780 IF A(X + 1, Y + 1) = 1 OR A(X + 1, Y - 1) = 1 THEN GOTO
     2600
1790 IF A(X + 1, Y + 1) = 1 AND A(X + 1, Y - 1) = 1 THEN
     GOTO 2600
1800 IF A(X + 1, Y - 1) = 1 THEN GOTO 2090
1810 IF A(X + 1, Y + 1) = 1 THEN GOTO 1490
1820 IF A(X + 1, Y) = 1 THEN GOTO 3000
1830 IF X = 9 THEN GOTO 1860
1840 LET X = X + 1
1850 GOTO 1790
1860 LET L1 = 19 - 2*(Y - 1)
1870 LET C1 = 19
1880 GOTO 4000
2000 REM**MOVING NORTH
2010 LET X = 26 - N
2020 LET Y = 1
2030 LET L = 19
2040 LET C = 2 + 2*(X - 1)
2050 PRINT AT L, C; S$
2060 FOR J = 1 TO 30
2070 NEXT J
2075 IF  A(X, 2) = 1 THEN GOTO 3000
2080 IF A(X - 1, Y + 1) = 1 OR A(X + 1, Y + 1) = 1 THEN GOTO
     2600
2090 IF A(X + 1, Y + 1) = 1 AND A(X - 1, Y + 1) = 1 THEN GOTO
     2600
2100 IF A(X + 1, Y + 1) = 1 THEN GOTO 2390
2110 IF A(X - 1, Y + 1) = 1 THEN GOTO 1790
2120 IF A(X, Y + 1) = 1 THEN GOTO 3000
2130 IF Y = 9 THEN GOTO 2160
2140 LET Y = Y + 1
2150 GOTO 2090
2160 LET L1 = 2
2170 LET C1 = 2 + 2*(X- 1)
2180 GOTO 4000
2300 REM * * MOVING WEST
2310 LET X = 10
2320 LET Y = 18 - N
2330 LET L = 19 - 2*(Y - 1)
2340 LET C = 19
2350 PRINT AT  L, C; S$
```

```
2360 FOR J = 1 TO 30
2370 NEXT J
2375 IF  A(9, Y) = 1 THEN GOTO 3000
2380 IF A(X - 1, Y + 1) = 1 OR A(X - 1, Y- 1) = 1
     THEN GOTO 2600
2390 IF A(X - 1, Y + 1) = 1 AND A(X - 1, Y - 1) = 1 THEN GOTO
     2600
2400 IF A(X - 1, Y + 1) = 1 THEN GOTO 1490
2410 IF A(X - 1, Y - 1) = 1 THEN GOTO 2090
2420 IF A(X - 1, Y) = 1 THEN GOTO 3000
2430 IF X = 2 THEN GOTO 2460
2440 LET X = X - 1
2450 GOTO 2390
2460 LET L1 = 19 - 2*(Y - 1)
2470 LET C1 = 2
2480 GOTO 4000
2600 REM**REFLECTION
2605 FOR J = 1 TO 10
2610 PRINT AT L, C; " "          (1 space)
2620 FOR K = 1 TO 2
2630 NEXT K
2640 PRINT AT L, C; "▒"          (1 GRAPHICS SHIFT A)
2650 FOR K = 1 TO 3
2660 NEXT K
2670 NEXT J
2680 RETURN
3000 REM**ABSORPTION
3010 FOR J = 1 TO 10
3020 PRINT AT L, C; " "          (1 space)
3030 FOR K = 1 TO 2
3040 NEXT K
3050 PRINT AT L, C; "*"
3060 FOR K = 1 TO 3
3070 NEXT K
3080 NEXT J
3090 RETURN
3300 REM**CLEARING TOP RIGHT SCREEN
3310 PRINT AT 0, 21; "  "        (2 spaces)
3320 FOR J = 0 TO 21
3330 PRINT AT J, 23; B$
3340 NEXT J
3350 RETURN
```

```
3600 REM**GUESSING AN ATOM
3610 PRINT AT 0, 23; "WHERE IS"; TAB 23; "THE ATOM?"
3620 PAUSE 200
3630 PRINT AT 3, 24; "SQUARES"; TAB 24 ; "ALONG?"
3635 GOSUB 4200
3640 LET X = VAL I$
3645 IF X > 8 THEN GOTO 3635
3650 PRINT X
3660 PAUSE 50
3670 PRINT AT 6, 25; "SQUARES"; TAB 27; "UP?";
3675 GOSUB 4200
3680 LET Y = VAL I$
3685 IF Y > 8 THEN GOTO 3675
3690 PRINT Y
3700 IF A(X + 1, Y + 1) = 1 THEN GOTO 3800
3710 PRINT AT 21 - 2*(Y + 1), 2*(X + 1); "0"          (inverse 0)
3720 PRINT AT 9, 25; "NO ATOM"; TAB 26; "THERE"
3730 PAUSE 200
3740 PRINT AT 12, 24; "PENALTY"; TAB 25; "3 SHOTS"
3750 LET NS = NS + 3
3760 PAUSE 200
3770 GOTO 240
3800 PRINT AT 21 - 2*(Y + 1), 2*(X + 1); "*"
     (inverse *)
3810 PRINT AT 10, 23; "WELL DONE"; TAB 24; "GOT ONE"
3820 PAUSE 300
3830 LET RG = RG + 1
3840 IF RG = 4 THEN GOTO 4300
3850 GOTO 240
3900 REM**SIGNING OFF
3920 PRINT AT 20,24;"PRESS";TAB 24;"ENTER"
3925 INPUT C$
3930 CLS
3940 PRINT AT 5, 0; "I HOPE YOU ENJOYED THE GAME",,
     TAB 10; "PLAY AGAIN SOME TIME"
3950 STOP
4000 REM**FLASHING LETTERS
4010 FOR J = 1 TO 10
4020 PRINT AT L, C; " "      (1 space)
4030 PRINT AT L1, C1; " "      (1 space)
4060 PRINT AT L, C; S$
4070 PRINT AT L1, C1; S$
```

```
4080 FOR K = 1 TO 3
4090 NEXT K
4100 NEXT J
4110 RETURN
4200 REM * GETTING AN INKEY$
4210 IF INKEY$ <> "" THEN GOTO 4210
4220 IF INKEY$ = "" THEN GOTO 4220
4230 LET I$ = INKEY$
4240 RETURN
4300 REM**CONGRATS
4310 GOSUB 3300
4320 PRINT AT 0,24;"YOU GOT";TAB 24;"THE LOT"
4330 PAUSE 100
4340 PRINT AT 3,24;"WITH THE";TAB 25;NS;"TH";TAB
     26; "SHOT"
4350 PAUSE 300
4360 PRINT AT 8,26;"PLAY";TAB 25;"AGAIN?";TAB 25;" ";
     TAB 25; "Y/N?"
4370 INPUT C$
4380 IF C$ = "Y" THEN RUN
4390 IF C$ = "N" THEN GOTO 3930
4400 GOTO 4370
```

LIST OF VARIABLES

A(10,10)	the 64 squares in the black box, plus an invisible line of squares all around the perimeter.
B$	a string of 9 spaces.
NS	the number of the current shot.
RG	the number of right guesses so far.
J,K	loop control variables.
I$	the current value of INKEY$.
S$	the current character indicating the beam in/beam out positions.
S	the code of this current character.
X,Y	grid coordinates.
L,C	line and column for printing character showing beam in.
L1,C1	line and column for printing character showing beam out.
C$	input string to make program continue.

LIST OF SUBROUTINES

1000	draws the grid with surrounding numbers.
1200	places the four atoms in the grid at random.
1300	prints the four atoms on the grid when player gives up.
1400	deals with beams moving south.
1700	deals with beams moving east.
2000	deals with beams moving north.
2300	deals with beams moving west.
2600	prints characters to show a reflection.
3000	prints characters to show an absorption.
3300	clears the top right part of the screen.
3600	asks player to guess the position of one atom, and checks whether guess is correct.
3900	end of game, signing off.
4000	flashes characters to show where beam has entered and left the box.
4200	puts the current value for **INKEY$** into **I$.**
4300	congratulations — players had guessed all four atoms

NOTES

The vital core of the program is made up of the four "moving" subroutines that are all very similar. These notes apply to the "moving east" subroutine:

Lines 1710 to 1720	set the coordinates for the starting point of the beam.
Lines 1730 to 1740	set the print position for the character showing the entry point of the beam.
Line 1775	checks for an edge absorption.
Line 1780	checks for an edge reflection.
Line 1790	checks for an internal reflection.
Line 1800	checks for an atom on the line below the entry point, which deflects the beam north.
Line 1810	checks for an atom on the line above the entry point, which deflects the beam south.
Line 1820	checks for an atom in the next square ahead, which gives an absorption.
Line 1830	checks whether the beam has gone right through the box.

Lines 184Ø to 185Ø	if the beam is still in the box, increase the X coordinate by one, and back to check everything once more.
Lines 186Ø to 188Ø	set the print position for the character showing the exit point of the beam, and off to 4ØØØ to flash the characters at entry and exit points.

14. TELEPHONE LIST (16K)

This is a domestic example of a database program. It is capable of holding a lot of numbered items of data in an array, in this case names and phone numbers up to a total of 20 characters per item. *The program must never be executed by the command RUN* — this would lose all the data you have put in. Always execute the program with **GOTO** 1ØØ. You will then be offered the choice of listing the items, putting a new item in, finding one item, or rubbing out an item. In each of the last three operations, the ZX81 is using only the first three characters of the items, so that "Find Norman" would also turn up Norton, North, Norden, etc.

You can alter the program to deal with any other information you want to store. You can change the number of items or their length, being limited to about 650 items of 20 characters in 16K of RAM.

```
  1Ø DIM N$(1ØØ, 2Ø)
  2Ø LET N$(1ØØ) = "END"
  3Ø LET E$ = "                    " (20 spaces)
 1ØØ CLS
 11Ø PRINT "PHONE NUMBER LIST",,,,,"ORDERS PLEASE?",,,,"LIST
     ALL THE NAMES = L", "PUT NEW NAME/NUMBER IN = N",
     "FIND A NUMBER = F", "REMOVE A NAME/NUMBER = R"
 12Ø INPUT Z$
 13Ø IF Z$ = "N" THEN GOTO 5ØØ
 14Ø IF Z$ = "F" THEN GOTO 2ØØ
 15Ø IF Z$ = "R" THEN GOTO 7ØØ
 16Ø IF Z$ = "L" THEN GOTO 4ØØ
 17Ø GOTO 12Ø
 2ØØ CLS
 2Ø5 PRINT,,,,"NAME PLEASE?"
 21Ø INPUT Z$
```

```
215 IF LEN Z$ < 3 THEN GOTO 210
220 LET F = 0
230 LET X = 1
240 CLS
250 IF N$(X, TO 3) <> Z$(TO 3) THEN GOTO 300
260 LET F = 1
270 PRINT,,N$(X)
300 LET X = X + 1
310 IF N$(X, TO 3) <> "END" THEN GOTO 250
320 IF F = 0 THEN PRINT Z$;"NOT FOUND"
330 GOTO 1000
400 CLS
410 LET X = 0
420 LET X = X + 1
430 SCROLL
440 PRINT N$(X)
450 IF N$(X, TO 3) <> "END" THEN GOTO 420
460 SCROLL
470 GOTO 1000
500 CLS
510 LET X = 1
520 IF N$(X, TO 3) = "END" THEN GOTO 570
530 IF N$(X) = E$ THEN GOTO 600
540 LET X = X + 1
550 GOTO 520
570 PRINT,,"SORRY — NO MORE ROOM"
580 GOTO 1000
600 CLS
610 PRINT "NEW NAME/NUMBER?"
620 INPUT N$(X)
630 GOTO 100
700 CLS
710 PRINT "REMOVE WHICH NAME?"
720 INPUT Z$
730 LET X = 1
735 IF N$(X, TO 3) = "END" THEN GOTO 850
740 IF N$(X, TO 3) <> Z$(TO 3) THEN GOTO 900
745 CLS
750 PRINT N$(X)
760 PRINT "PRESS R TO REMOVE",,,"OR ENTER FOR NEXT";
    Z$(TO 3)
770 INPUT R$
```

```
780 IF R$ <> "R" THEN GOTO 900
790 PRINT,,N$(X);' REMOVED"
800 LET N$(X) = E$
810 GOTO 1000
850 CLS
860 PRINT,,"NO MORE";Z$(TO 3);"NAMES IN THE LIST"
870 GOTO 1000
900 LET X = X + 1
910 GOTO 735
1000 PRINT AT 21, 13;"PRESS N/L FOR MORE"
1010 INPUT Z$
1020 GOTO 100
```

LIST OF VARIABLES

N$ (100,20)	array of 100 strings of 20 characters each.
Z$,R$	input string variables.
F	flag to indicate whether or not name found.
X	current subscript number.

NOTES

Lines 100 to 170	print a menu of four possible choices, with program branching in four different directions.
Lines 200 to 330	routine for finding a name/number. Since only the first three letters have to match, this can turn up more than one name.
Lines 400 to 470	produce scrolled list of all the 100 names in subscript order.
Lines 500 to 630	search for the first empty member of the array, and then allow the user to insert a new name.
Lines 700 to 910	routine for rubbing out an existing name. The user types in the name he wishes to rub out, and the program produces all the names corresponding (first three letters) one by one, with the option of deleting or going on to the next.

APPENDIX 4

Sample Answers to Exercises

PROGRAMS

There are plenty of ways of writing a computer program. Do note that these are sample answers, and that they only use computer instructions learned up to the chapter concerned. Your own solutions may be different but just as correct.

EXERCISE 6.1. LINE CHANGING

Type 15, **ENTER**,20,**ENTER**, and then:

```
10 PRINT "THREE LINES GONE, ONE LEFT"
```

EXERCISE 6.2. YOUR ADDRESS

NEW deletes the old program.

```
1000 PRINT "MR. JOHN SMITH"
2000 PRINT " 23 HANLEY ROAD"
3000 PRINT " STAFFORD"
4000 PRINT "  SD23 6MX"
```

EXERCISE 7.1. EXPRESSIONS WITH PARENTHESES

(1) Stage 1 7 − 5 = 2 30 / 12 = 2.5
Stage 2 2*2.5 = 5
Stage 3 5**3 = 125 (answer)

(2) Stage 1 6*8 = 48 23 − 11 = 12
Stage 2 48 − 12 = 36 5 + 7 = 12
Stage 3 36 / 12 = 3
Stage 4 3**2 = 9 (answer)

EXERCISE 8.1. MONEY CHANGING

```
10 LET R = 1.9
20 LET P = 75
30 LET D = 250
40 PRINT P*R
50 PRINT "US DOLLARS FOR"
60 PRINT P
70 PRINT "£"
100 PRINT
110 PRINT
120 PRINT D / R
130 PRINT "£ NEEDED TO GET"
140 PRINT D
150 PRINT "US DOLLARS"
```

EXERCISE 8.2. PARACHUTING

```
10 LET T = 22
20 LET A = 9.8
30 LET H = 3000 - A*T**2 / 2
40 PRINT "TIME ="
50 PRINT T
60 PRINT
70 PRINT "HEIGHT ="
80 PRINT H
```

The height is 2510 m after 10 seconds. If you put various times into line 1Ø, you will find that after 22 seconds free fall the height is 628 m; that's the time to pull the rip cord.

EXERCISE 9.1. CIRCLES

```
 1Ø LET R = 5
 2Ø LET D = 2*R
 3Ø LET C = 3.14*D
 4Ø LET A = R**2*3.14
 5Ø PRINT "  VITAL STATISTICS OF A CIRCLE"
 6Ø PRINT
 7Ø PRINT "IF THE RADIUS IS";R;"IN"
 8Ø PRINT
 9Ø PRINT "DIAM =";D;"IN", "CIRCUMF = ";C;"IN"
1ØØ PRINT TAB 8;"AREA =";A;"SQ IN"
```

EXERCISE 11.1. DECIMAL PART

```
1Ø LET N = 17.59
2Ø PRINT "NUMBER";TAB 1Ø;"INT";TAB 2Ø;"DECIMAL"
3Ø PRINT
4Ø PRINT N;TAB 1Ø;INT N;TAB 2Ø;N - INT N
```

EXERCISE 11.2. MORE ROUNDING

```
1Ø LET N = 2.75
2Ø PRINT INT (N*1Ø + .5) / 1Ø
```

EXERCISE 12.1. BUILDING INTEREST ON SAVINGS

```
 2Ø LET C = 5ØØ
 3Ø LET Y = 1982
1ØØ PRINT Y;"CAPITAL + INTEREST = $";C
11Ø PRINT
```

```
120 LET Y = Y + 1
130 LET C = C*1.08
140 IF Y < 1990 THEN GOTO 100
```

Change line 100 as follows to round off to the nearest p.

```
100 PRINT Y;"CAPITAL + INTEREST = $"; INT (C*100 + .5) / 100
```

EXERCISE 12.2. WHEN ARE THE LEAP YEARS?

```
 10 LET Y = 1982
100 PRINT "YEAR"
110 PRINT Y;
120 IF Y / 4 = INT (Y / 4) THEN PRINT "LEAP YEAR";
130 LET Y = Y + 1
140 PRINT
150 IF Y < 2000 THEN GOTO 110
```

EXERCISE 14.1. PERCENTAGES

```
10 PRINT "YOUR MARK?";
20 INPUT M
30 PRINT M,,,, "MAX POSS MARK?"
40 INPUT MAX
50 CLS
60 PRINT M;"OUT OF";MAX;" = ";M/MAX*100;"PER CENT"
70 GOTO 10
```

EXERCISE 14.2. GASOLINE CONSUMPTION

```
10 PRINT "HOW MANY MILES?";
20 INPUT M
30 PRINT M
40 PRINT "GALLONS USED?"
50 INPUT G
60 CLS
```

```
70 PRINT G;"GALL FOR";M;"MILES = "; M / G;" M.P.G.""
80 PRINT
90 GOTO 10
```

EXERCISE 16.1. TABLE OF SQUARE ROOTS

```
 10 PRINT "NUMBER", "SQUARE ROOT"
 20 PRINT
100 FOR N = 0 TO 16
110 PRINT N,SQR N
120 NEXT N
```

EXERCISE 16.2. MULTIPLES OF FOUR

```
10 PRINT "MULTIPLES OF 4 UP TO 100"
20 FOR J = 0 TO 100 STEP 4
30 PRINT TAB 2*J;J;
40 NEXT J
```

EXERCISE 17.1. MULTIPLICATION SQUARE

```
10 FOR J = 1 TO 7
20 FOR K = 1 TO 7
30 PRINT TAB 4*K;J*K;
40 NEXT K
50 PRINT,,,,
60 NEXT J
```

EXERCISE 17.2. RECTANGLE

```
10 FOR J = 1 TO 5
20 FOR K = 1 TO 19
30 PRINT "■";
40 NEXT K
50 PRINT,,,,
60 NEXT J
```

For a title, change line 1Ø to:

```
10 FOR J = 1 TO 4
```

and add:

```
60 IF J = 2 THEN PRINT "THIS IS A RECTANGLE" (inverse letters)
```

EXERCISE 18.1. FORM FILLING

```
 10 PRINT "YOUR SURNAME PLEASE"
 20 INPUT S$
 30 PRINT,, "NOW YOUR FIRST NAME"
 40 INPUT F$
 50 PRINT,, "AGE IN YEARS PLEASE"
 60 INPUT A$
 70 PRINT,, "AND WHERE DO YOU LIVE?"
 80 INPUT T$
 90 CLS
100 PRINT "THANK YOU VERY MUCH";F$," ";S$
110 PRINT,, "YOU ARE";A$;"YEARS OLD"
120 PRINT "AND YOU LIVE IN";T$
```

EXERCISE 19.1. CHOOSING NUMBERS

```
 10 PRINT "TYPE A WHOLE NUMBER FROM 1 TO 99"
 20 PRINT " THEN PRESS ENTER"
 30 INPUT N
 40 IF N < 1 THEN GOTO 100
 50 IF N > 99 THEN GOTO 100
 60 IF N <> INT N THEN GOTO 200
 70 GOTO 300
100 PRINT "NUMBER FROM 1 TO 99 PLEASE"
110 GOTO 30
200 PRINT "WHOLE NUMBERS PLEASE"
```

```
210 GOTO 30
300 CLS
310 PRINT "YOUR NUMBER IS";N
320 PRINT,,,, "ITS SQUARE IS"; N*N
330 PRINT,,,,,, "NEXT NUMBER?"
340 GOTO 30
```

Note: At present you cannot guard against the user putting in letters — these give a 2/30 error. To cover this you need to know about the statement **VAL** which comes later.

EXERCISE 20.1. ROULETTE

```
100 LET S = INT (RND * 37)
110 IF S < 10 THEN PRINT " ";
120 PRINT S;"";          (2 spaces)
130 GOTO 100
```

Note: As written here the program includes a single zero, which I believe is the usual thing.

EXERCISE 20.2. RANDOM RECTANGLES

```
100 LET N = INT (RND*15 + 1)
200 FOR J = 1 TO INT (RND*15 + 1)
210 FOR K = 1N
220 PRINT "▒";          (one GRAPHICS SHIFT A)
230 NEXT K
240 PRINT
250 NEXT J
300 PAUSE 50
310 CLS
320 GOTO 200
```

EXERCISE 21.1. WATER TANK VOLUMES

```
 10 LET V = 0
110 PRINT,,,, "WHAT SHAPE IS IT?"
```

```
 120 PRINT,, "CYLINDER — TYPE CYL"
 130 PRINT" OR CUBE — TYPE CUBE"
 140 INPUT A$
 150 CLS
 160 IF A$ = "CYL" THEN GOSUB 1000
 170 IF A$ = "CUBE" THEN GOSUB 2000
 180 IF V <> 0 THEN GOTO 300
 190 PRINT "DONT KNOW";A$;"SHAPE"
 200 GOTO 140
 300 PRINT "VOL OF";A$; " = ";V;" CUBIC IN"
 900 STOP
1000 REM**VOL OF CYL
1010 PRINT "HEIGHT IN IN?"
1020 INPUT H
1030 PRINT H,,,, "DIAM IN IN?";
1040 INPUT D
1050 PRINT D
1060 LET V = PI*(D/2)**2*H
1070 RETURN
2000 REM*VOL OF CUBE
2010 PRINT "EDGE LENGTH IN IN?";
2020 INPUT E
2030 PRINT E
2040 LET V = E**3
2050 RETURN
```

Note: In line 180 we are using V as a flag to make the ZX81 by-pass lines 190 and 200 if the volume has been calculated.

EXERCISE 22.1. NUMBER GUESSING

```
 20 PRINT "WHATS MY CODE (10 TO 99)", "YOU HAVE 8
    GUESSES"
100 LET C = INT (RND*90 + 10)
130 FOR J = 1 TO 8
140 PRINT "GUESS";J;"?"
145 PAUSE 150
150 LET G$ = " "
200 FOR K = 1 TO 2
210 IF INKEY$ <> " " THEN GOTO 210
220 IF INKEY$ = " " THEN GOTO 220
```

```
230 PRINT INKEY$;
240 LET G$ = G$ + INKEY$
250 NEXT K
310 LET G = VAL G$
320 IF G = C THEN GOTO 500
330 IF G > C THEN GOTO 370
340 PRINT "IS TOO LOW"
350 GOTO 400
370 PRINT "IS TOO HIGH"
400 NEXT J
450 PRINT,,  "IT WAS";C
460 STOP
500 PRINT "IS RIGHT"
510 PRINT "GUESSED IT IN";J"GOES"
```

Note: In line 150 we have to reset G$ to " ", the empty string, in order to get rid of the previous guess.

EXERCISE 23.1. VERTICAL LINES

```
100 FOR K = 0 TO 43
110 PLOT 0,K
120 PLOT 63,K
130 NEXT K
```

Note: The program will not complete the verticals because of shortage of memory — you are trying to use too much screen. You must reduce the height from 43 to 37 to get a complete rectangle.

EXERCISE 23.2. CALLING CARD

```
 10 FOR J = 12 TO 50
 20 FOR K = 16 TO 30
 30 PLOT J,K
 40 NEXT K
 50 NEXT J
100 PRINT AT 8,8;"JOHN JONES ESQ.,";TAB 9;"21 OXFORD
    ROAD"; TAB 10;"CHISWICK";TAB 12;"W.4."        (all
    inverse letters)
```

Note: In line 100, **PRINT AT** 8,8 sets the print position on the first line; and then **TAB** is used to skip on to succeeding lines.

EXERCISE 23.3. "ON WE GO" SUBROUTINE

```
 100 PRINT "PAUSING NOW"
 110 GOSUB 1000
 120 PRINT AT 5,0;"GOING ON AGAIN"
 900 STOP
1000 REM**ON WE GO
1010 PRINT AT 21,19;"PRESS ENTER"
1020 INPUT A$
1030 PRINT AT 21,19;"             "      (13 spaces)
1040 RETURN
```

EXERCISE 24.1. ANTS

```
 10 LET L = 5
 20 LET C = 0
 30 PRINT "WHATS AN ANT?"
 40 PAUSE 300
100 PRINT AT 0,0;"TYPE A WORD          " (32 letters plus
          spaces)
110 INPUT W$
120 IF LEN W$ < 3 THEN GOTO 200
130 IF W$ (1 TO 3) = "ANT" THEN GOTO 300
140 IF W$ (LEN W$ - 2 TO LEN W$) = "ANT" THEN GOTO 300
200 PRINT AT 0,0;W$;"IS NOT AN ANT"
210 GOTO 40
300 PRINT AT 3,5;"LIST OF ANTS"
310 PRINT AT L,C;W$
320 LET L = L + SGN C
330 LET C = 15 - C
340 GOTO 100
```

Notes: Line 120 rejects words of less than three letters.
Lines 130 and 140 accept words with ANT at the beginning or the end of the word.

Line 320 increases the **PRINT** line number by 1 on alternate loops.
Line 330 sets the **PRINT** column to 0 and 15 alternately.

EXERCISE 25.1. SIMPLE COWS AND BULLS

```
 10 RAND
 20 DIM N(4)
 30 LET B = 0
100 FOR J = 1 TO 4
110 LET N(J) = INT (RND*6 + 1)
120 NEXT J
200 PRINT "GUESS MY NUMBER", "FOUR DIGITS ALL BETWEEN 1
    AND 6"
210 INPUT A$
220 CLS
230 PRINT "YOUR GUESS WAS  ";A$
300 FOR J = 1 TO 4
310 IF N(J) = VAL A$(J) THEN LET B = B + 1
320 NEXT J
400 PRINT,,, "YOU SCORED ";B;"  BULLS"
```

Note: A program for the complete game is listed in Appendix 3, but maybe you would like to try your own hand at one first.

EXERCISE 26.1. TEST RESULTS

```
 10 DIM C$(6, 6)
 20 DIM M(6)
100 LET C$(1) = "SIMON"
110 LET C$(2) = "MARINA"
120 LET C$(3) = "WILLIAM"
130 LET C$(4) = "EMILY"
140 LET C$(5) = "JAMES"
150 LET C$(6) = "JOANNE"
200 PRINT "NAME OF TEST?"
210 INPUT T$
220 PRINT T$,"MAX MARK?";
230 INPUT M
```

```
240 PRINT M
300 FOR J = 1 TO 6
310 PRINT C$(J),"MARK?";
320 INPUT M(J)
330 PRINT M(J)
340 NEXT J
400 CLS
410 PRINT T$;"TEST",,,,
420 PRINT "NAME", "PER CENT",,,
430 FOR J = 1 TO 6
440 PRINT C$(J), M(J)*100 / M
450 NEXT J
```

Note: Here we have two parallel single-dimension arrays, one for the names and one for the marks, in order to save memory. In a 16K program for a full class, one might use a two-dimension string array, input the marks as strings, and use **VAL** to turn them into numbers.

EXERCISE 26.2. ONE-ARMED BANDIT

```
 10 RAND
 20 DIM W$(6,6)
 30 DIM N(3)
100 LET W$(1) = "BELL"
110 LET W$(2) = "LEMON"
120 LET W$(3) = "JOKER"
130 LET W$(4) = "ANCHOR"
140 LET W$(5) = "CHERRY"
150 LET W$(6) = "APPLE"
200 FOR J = 1 TO 3
210 LET N(J) = INT (RND*6 +)
220 PRINT AT 10,(J - 1)*12;W$(N(J))
230 NEXT J
240 IF N(1) <> N(2) THEN GOTO 300
250 IF N(2) <> N(3) THEN GOTO 300
260 PRINT AT 18,15;"JACKPOT"
270 STOP
300 INPUT A$
310 GOTO 200
```

Note: Here we have a single-dimension array of six strings, and one of three random numbers. In line 220 we are using a member of the number array as the subscript to the string array variable. Lines 240-250 are not very elegant, we need logical AND which comes in the next chapter.

EXERCISE 27.1. WATER TANK MK.2

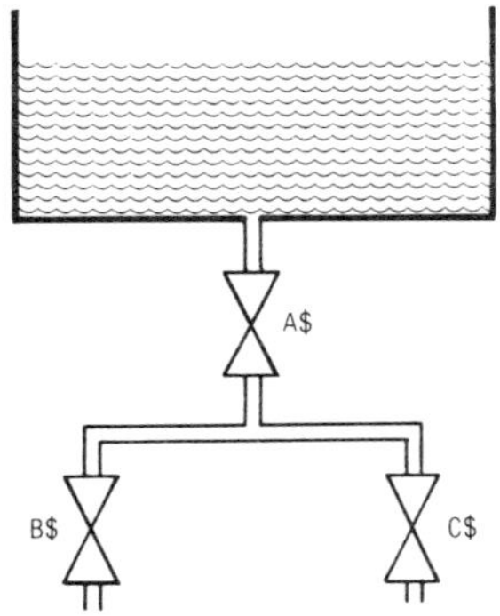

Note: Water will only run out of the tank if tap A$ is open, as well as either tap B$ or tap C$.

EXERCISE 28.1. FLASHER

```
 100 GOSUB 1000
 900 STOP
1000 REM**FLASHING WINNER
1010 FOR J = 1 TO 10
1020 PRINT AT 21,15;"      "      (6 spaces)
1030 FOR K = 1 TO 10
1040 NEXT K
1050 PRINT AT 21,15;"WINNER"      (inverse letters)
1060 FOR K = 1 TO 20
1070 NEXT K
1080 NEXT J
1090 RETURN
```

EXERCISE 28.2. RUBBER BALL

```
 10 LET V = Ø
 20 LET VV = 1
100 FOR J = 2Ø TO 4Ø
110 PLOT J,1
120 NEXT J
140 FOR X = Ø TO 19
150 PRINT AT V,15;" "
160 LET V = V + VV
170 PRINT AT V,15;"0"
180 IF V = X OR V = 2Ø THEN LET VV = -VV
190 IF V <> 2Ø THEN GOTO 15Ø
200 NEXT X
```

EXERCISE 28.3. LUNAR MODULE

```
100 FOR L = Ø TO 18
110 PRINT AT L,15;" ";TAB 14;"A";TAB 14;"<S>";TAB 14;
    "| |"
120 FOR K = Ø TO L*2
130 NEXT K
140 NEXT L
```

Note: All the strings making up the module are three characters long, and the "S" in the middle should be inverse. The module is an unshamed steal from "Lunar Landing," an excellent game — one of a series produced in cassette form by Sinclair ZX Software.

Lines 12Ø and 13Ø provide a steadily increasing pause in the main loop, to make the landing reasonably soft.

APPENDIX 5

Expanding Your ZX81 Memory to 16K

The main part of this book has been written for users of the Sinclair ZX81 (and generally for the ZX80 with BASIC in 8K ROM) with the standard 1K of RAM or user memory in which to put program, data, display file, and so on. As your programming technique improves, you will soon find that you need more RAM than this. Sinclair Research Ltd. supplies a neat expansion box that plugs into the edge connector at the back of the ZX81/ZX80 to provide a total of 16K of RAM. At a little more than two thirds of the cost of the assembled ZX81, it represents good value by today's standards.

The expanded ZX81 can be used to write longer programs (such as Program 13 in Appendix 3). It can also be used to store more data, remembering that all data is saved on tape with your program, and can be loaded and used again later (Programs 9 and 14 in Appendix 3).

The 16K RAM Pack is no problem to use — simply plug it in *before* you switch the power on (never insert it or remove it while the ZX81 is turned on). Remember, even short programs saved with the 16K RAM Pack in place take up more tape space — it's best to plug in the Pack again when you want to load them later.

THE 16K RAM PACK BEING INSERTED INTO THE ZX81

Index

TO THE READER

Sams Computer books cover Fundamentals — Programming — Interfacing — Technology written to meet the needs of computer engineers, professionals, scientists, technicians, students, educators, business owners, personal computerists and home hobbyists.

Our Tradition is to meet your needs and in so doing we invite you to tell us what your needs and interests are by completing the following:

1. I need books on the following topics:

____

____

____

____

____

____

2. I have the following Sams titles:

____

____

____

____

____

____

3. My occupation is:

_____ Scientist, Engineer

_____ Personal computerist

_____ Technician, Serviceman

_____ Educator

_____ Student

_____ D P Professional

_____ Business owner

_____ Computer store owner

_____ Home hobbyist

Other ______________________

____

Name (print) ______________________________________

Address ______________________________________

City ____________________ State ____________ Zip ____________

Mail to: **Howard W. Sams & Co., Inc.**
Marketing Dept. #CBS1/80
4300 W. 62nd St., P.O. Box 7092
Indianapolis, Indiana 46206

21957